THE WORLD'S ELITE FORCES
ARMS AND EQUIPMENT

GREENHILL MILITARY MANUALS

THE WORLD'S ELITE FORCES
ARMS AND EQUIPMENT

WILL FOWLER

ILLUSTRATED BY RAY HUTCHINS

GREENHILL MILITARY MANUALS

Greenhill Books, London

Stackpole Books, Pennsylvania

This edition of **The World's Elite Forces: Arms and Equipment**
published 2001 by
Greenhill Books, Lionel Leventhal Limited, Park House,
1 Russell Gardens, London NW11 9NN
www.greenhillbooks.com
and
Stackpole Books, 5067 Ritter Road, Mechanicsburg, PA 17055, USA

British Library Cataloguing in Publication Data
Fowler, William, 1947–
The world's elite forces: arms and equipment. – Rev. ed. – (Greenhill military manuals)
1. Special forces (Military science) – Equipment and supplies
I. Title II. Hutchins, Ray
355.8

ISBN 1-85367-495-8

Library of Congress Cataloging-in-Publication Data available

Publishing History
The World's Elite Forces: Arms and Equipment was first published by Greenhill Books in 1996 as **Arms and Equipment of Special Forces.** The text of the first edition is here reproduced, complete and unabridged.

Original edition typeset by Merlin Publications; revisions by John Anastasio, Creative Line
Printed in Singapore by Kyodo Printing Company

The cover illustration shows a Pilkington Eagle night-vision sight, paired with a Simrad laser imagefinder, courtesy of Pilkington PE Ltd.

Introduction

Special Forces have always had an allure which is absent with more conventional infantry, artillery or armour. Their numbers are normally small, because to join them a soldier must pass rigorous selection courses as well as continuation training. They will usually have service in the regular forces before they opt for duty in Special Forces and are therefore normally older, around 28-30, compared to the average soldier in his teens and twenties. Special Forces remain, then, essentially a 'super force' which has taken many of the basic fighting skills and refined them to very high levels.

Though they may be able to patrol for long periods, in hostile territory, or reach forward Observation Posts (OP) on foot, they may be delivered to the operational area by fixed or rotary wing aircraft, or even drive into action themselves using lightweight trucks or motor-cycles and even cruise in using specialised small boats.

Contrary to images on film or television, Special Forces avoid non-regular weapons and clothing and even forbear wearing long hair and moustaches. These characteristic 'signatures' or indicators may attract attention and identify the users as Special Forces in hostile territory even before they have been inserted into an operational area.

Non-regular issue weapons and equipment are usually avoided since they may require non-standard ammunition or batteries to operate, which can impose a burden on the logistic chain. Special Forces may, however, adopt the weapons used by their enemies so that the sound of firing and the presence of empty cartridge cases do not attract attention and they are also able to re-stock from captured sources. Captured or civilian footwear has also been used so that tracks are not obvious.

There is a case for some special weapons and equipment where these enhance the fire-power or performance of a small group. A notable example is in hostage rescue operations where the team will need to deliver a heavy volume of very accurate fire at short ranges. Satellite communications allow soldiers deep inside hostile territory to communicate with friendly aircraft or artillery to call in powerful indirect fire if they encounter large numbers of hostile forces

Global Positioning Systems (GPS) are widely used now on sea, in the air and on land by civilians and service personnel; whereas, only a few years ago, they were the reserve of wealthy yachtsmen and Special Forces. Together with a Laser Range Finder (LRF), a GPS allows a member of the Special Forces to give incredibly accurate target indications to fighter ground attack aircraft or artillery. Laser designators can then be used by Special Forces patrols to 'paint' a target for aircraft equipped with Laser Guided Bombs (LGB) which means that a 1000 lb bomb can be aimed to hit a target as small as a tank or truck.

Special Forces may also include amongst their equipment agricultural, construction and medical supplies, which are used in 'hearts and minds' operations with rural communities. The construction of schools, hospitals and dispensaries, administration of medicine, as well as the improvement of crop yields and agricultural practice, may be a more effective way of winning a low intensity counter-revolutionary campaign, than would ambushes and patrols.

The type of men who can work in small groups, handle sophisticated communications equipment, have almost instant reactions in a fire-fight, have the courage to jump into hostile territory by parachute or land in the dark on an alien coast, in foul weather conditions and who are also able to turn their hand to river-fishing and paediatrics amongst simple rural communities are 'Special Forces' indeed!

Contents

The Future

Though the Cold War may be over and the need for defence against a Communist threat is no longer with us there is still a highly important role for Special Forces.

Tribalism and religious extremism have replaced Communism as a threat to national stability and the revenue made from narcotics is as great as the budgets of many emerging nations. Urban terrorism with bombings, murder or hijacks, or rural campaigns moving between conventional and unconventional warfare, are, and will be, the scenes of involvement for Special Forces and, with their emphasis on covert operations, they are ideal soldiers for enforcing government foreign policy. They can be inserted as medical, military or farming training teams assisting the forces of foreign governments that are under internal or external threat and in this role a team can move easily into direct action if intelligence presents a lucrative target. In a country under attack by drug cartels Special Forces teams, training the local police and army, may use this role as a cover to attack key figures in the cartel leadership. In hijacks, the kidnappers may aim to take an aircraft to a friendly or at least neutral airport; an attack on this aircraft by Special Forces is therefore an operation fraught with diplomatic traps; however, it is an accepted convention that rescues are carried out by soldiers or Special Forces from the hostages' country of origin.

Good intelligence is vital. Terrorist profiles, plans of buildings or layouts of aircraft, held in central computers, can be sent as data via satellite links to governments or Special Forces teams. Modern communications systems are necessary to allow a plan to be cleared at the highest government level and for senior politicians to be kept informed. Given the speed of satellite news coverage, Special Forces are able to send an "after action" report within minutes of the operation being completed. On the ground Special Forces are under pressure to keep collateral damage to a minimum.

On 1st August 1996 a new special force, the Joint Rapid Deployment Force (JRDF), was launched to provide the SPEARHEAD Battalion to NATO's Allied Command Europe Mobile Force and the United Kingdom contribution to the ACE Mobile Force. The JRDF relies on a central core, provided by 3 Commando Brigade and 5 Airborne Brigade, supported by units assigned from the National Contingency Forces of all three services, which will be able to assemble and deploy a force of up to reinforced Brigade strength, tailored specifically to meet the demands of individual operations. Within the JRDF are the special forces of the SAS and SBS to form the ADVANCE FORCE OPERATIONS Group who would be inserted covertly into theatre by air or sea. They will form a Special Force within a Special Force!

The versatility of the Special Forces of each nation and their level of training gives them a high military value They are tough and they are an asset to be husbanded. Special Forces in the 21st Century will be a force multiplier for the smaller professional armies that will be required to keep the peace and combat the forces of disorder.

ADVANCE FORCE OPERATIONS. This group, made up of Special Forces of the SAS and SBS can be inserted covertly into theatre by air (C-130/Chinook) or sea (submarine/Rigid Raider).

The JRDF will quickly react to execute Land, Maritime, Air, Logistic and Special Forces components in carrying out campaign plans under the command of the new Permanent Joint Headquarters (PJHQ).

The JRDF in action. A well-balanced, high-readiness force on short notice to move and provide the full range of capabilities for maritime, land and air operations, working as a coherent joint structure.

Browning 9 mm High Power Pistol   Belgium

The **Browning Grande Puissance (GP)** or High Power 9 mm pistol is still in service with over 50 countries world wide even though it traces its origins back to patents issued in the mid 1920s. During the war, Waffen-SS troops used weapons made at the Fabrique Nationale factory at Herstal, Belgium, while in Canada John Inglis set up a production line in Toronto for the Allies. The **Browning High Power** was popular with Commandos and the SAS. One of the attractions of the weapon is its staggered magazine which accommodates 13 rounds; most pistols and revolvers in the 1930s and 40s held only 6 to 8 rounds. Early versions made by Inglis for export to China were equipped with adjustable tangent sights and a detachable butt which locked onto the pistol grip.

The **GP** remained in service with the British Army and SAS after the war because it is so robust - the pistol frame is machined out of a solid block of steel. Though there can be misfeeds with unsuitable ammunition, it is a forgiving weapon which works even when fouled. When the ammunition has been expended the magazine follower forces up the slide stop so the slide is held open to the rear. When a fresh magazine has been inserted, the slide stop can be pressed down to allow the return spring to force the slide forward.

It is easy to field strip with six parts including the magazine; a workshop strip reduces the pistol to 56 parts. The ammunition is compatible with that used in the Sterling sub-machine gun and other 9 mm weapons.

The pistol has been modernised as the **HP Mk 2** with anatomical grip plates and an ambidextrous safety catch. The safety on the original weapon was on the left but could be operated by the right thumb if the firer was right handed. The Mark 3 improved the Mark 2 with features like a larger ejection port, and sights mounted on a dovetail for easier adjustment - it can be removed and replaced with target sights. The Mark 3 is still in production and though the weapon is heavier than more modern designs, which use glass reinforced polymer (GRP) and alloys, it is likely that the **Browning 9 mm** will continue in service into the 21st Century.

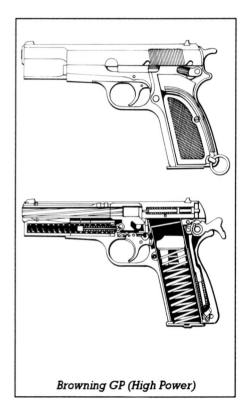

Browning GP (High Power)

10

Specification

Cartridge: 9 mm Parabellum
Operating system: recoil semi-automatic
Weight, empty: 882 g
Length, overall: 200 mm
Barrel: 118 mm 6 grooves, rh
Feed system: 13 round box magazine
Muzzle velocity: 350 m/s
Manufacturer: FN Herstal, Voie de Liège 33, B-4040 Herstal, Belgium

An anonymous member of the Special Air Services with the old but reliable 9 mm Browning High Power pistol.

Universal Self-loading Pistol (USP)   Germany

The **Heckler & Koch Universal Self-loading Pistol**, or **USP**, was developed for the domestic market in the United States, but its potential as a military side arm was soon recognised in Europe and the USA. In the United States it has been selected and developed by the Special Operations Command (SOCOM) as the Offensive Handgun Weapon System (OHWS) for the US Navy SEALS, US Army Special Forces and Delta Force. The order from SOCOM calls for 7500 pistols and 2000 laser aiming modules and silencers. The laser aiming device places a small red dot on the target which makes instinctive shooting easier and allows the weapon to be fired accurately from the hip. The silencer has two benefits, both reducing noise and eliminating the muzzle flash which would give away the firer's position at night.

The **USP** is a modern design which uses alloys and glass reinforced polymer (GRP) in its construction. Buffering within the pistol reduces recoil forces and makes it easier to return to the aim after firing a round.

There has been considerable debate within the United States Armed Forces over the respective merits of 9 mm and .45 ammunition, and although 9 mm has been adopted as the standard pistol calibre, .45 ammunition still has its proponents. The USP resolves this debate since it can be chambered for .45, .40 or 9 mm ammunition.

The SOCOM pistol is in .45 calibre, since experience has shown that the bigger, slower round will knock a man down, but the smaller, faster 9 mm may pass through him.

When Col. Charles Beckwith was forming Delta Force he specified that they should be armed with the Colt .45 since in a hostage rescue operation the .45 is safer and a sure man-stopper.

In 9 mm the USP holds 15 rounds, in .40 in (S&W) it holds 13 rounds and in the .45 in (ACP) it holds 12 rounds. In German service the 9 mm version of the **USP** is known as the P8.

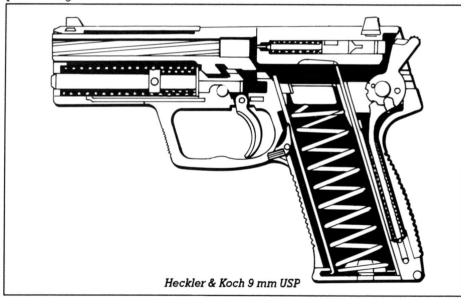

Heckler & Koch 9 mm USP

Specification

Cartridge: 9 mm x 19, .40 S&W, .45 ACP
Operating system: recoil, re-designed Browning action
Weight, empty: 9mm 720 g;
               .40 780 g;
               .45 783 g
Length: 194 mm (.45 200 mm)
Feed: box magazine 9 mm - 15;
               .40 - 13;
               .45 - 12 rounds
Manufacturer: Heckler & Koch GmbH, Obendorf-Neckar, Germany

The Heckler and Koch 9 mm Universal Self-loading Pistol in its three configurations: 9 mm, .40 ACP and .45 S&W. Though recoil forces are greater with the larger calibres, the buffer system still makes the pistol easier to handle than earlier weapons.

Uzi 9 mm Sub-machine Gun Israel

The **Uzi sub-machine gun** has been adopted by the armed forces of at least seven countries, and in its mini and micro designs is used by special forces and close protection teams. It was one of the weapons carried by Israeli paratroops in the successful Entebbe raid that freed hostages in July 1976. In 1981 when a would-be assassin attempted to kill President Ronald Reagan one of his body guards deployed an Uzi from a brief case. The Uzi was originally designed so that it could be made with a minimum of machined parts by light engineering companies, in Israel, in the years immediately after their War of Independence.

All the designs are based on the advanced blowback system in which the round is fired as the bolt is still travelling forward. This reduces the impulse on the bolt, which can consequently be almost half the weight of a static firing breech block. The magazine inserts into the pistol grip, which makes loading and unloading in the dark easier and the hollow pistol grip gives the magazine greater support. It uses a 25 or 32-round box magazine. Though there is a conventional change-lever with A for Automatic, R for single shot and S for Safe, the pistol grip has a grip safety catch which must be fully depressed before the gun will fire.

The cocking-lever is at the top of the weapon, which makes it easier for ambidextrous shooting, though left handers will find the ejection close to their face.

The standard weapon with a folding metal stock weighs 3.7 kg when empty and has a cyclic rate of fire of 600 rounds per minute (rpm). The Mini-Uzi weighs 2.70 kg when empty with a cyclic rate of 950 rpm. The pistol-like Micro-Uzi weighs 1.95 kg and has a rate of fire of 1250 rpm, with a 20-round magazine. It will fire 9 mm x 19 rounds or .45 ACP ammunition but this bigger round restricts magazine capacity to 16 shots. The folding wire stock allows the weapon to be kept under control when fired from the hip, since it can be held by the right arm against the firer's side.

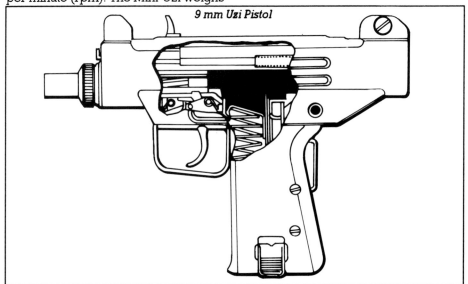

9 mm Uzi Pistol

Specification

Mini-Uzi

Cartridge: 9 mm Parabellum
Operating system: Blowback selective fire
Weight empty: 2.70 kg
Length, overall: 600 mm
Barrel: 197 mm
Feed system: 20, 25 and 32-round box magazines
Rate of fire: 950 rpm
Muzzle velocity: 352 m/s
Manufacturer: Israel Military Industries, Ramat Ha Sharon, Israel

A 9 mm Uzi sub-machine gun, as used by the German ACE Mobile Force. This picture shows the Uzi with the stock folded.

Steyr AUG 5.56 mm Rifle   Austria

When the **Steyr Armee Universal Gewehr (AUG)** was introduced into service with the Austrian Army in the late 1970s it caused considerable interest because of its novel bullpup design which uses plastics and has a built in x 1.5 optic sight in the carrying handle. The sights have been optimised for battle ranges and have a graticule which consists of a black ring in the field of view which can easily be placed on a man-sized target at 300 m. The bullpup configuration has working parts at the rear with the magazine behind the trigger. This may look and feel a little odd to soldiers familiar with weapons like the M16 or AK family of weapons, but it has the advantage that a full length rifle barrel can be fitted into a smaller space.

The clear plastic magazine on the **AUG** allows the soldier to check, at a glance, the supply of ammunition he holds. The weapon fires on singe-shot or automatic, but can be adjusted for a three-round burst as an alternative to single shots.

The **AUG** has been produced in four versions with the same mechanical features. The rifle has a 508 mm barrel and weighs 3.85 kg with a loaded magazine; the carbine weighs 3.65 kg with its 407 mm barrel; the sub-machine gun weighs 3.25 kg and has a 350 mm barrel and the heavy barrel version of the **AUG** has a 626 mm barrel, weighs 4.9 kg unloaded and has a light bipod and a 42-round magazine.

Accessories include a blank firing attachment, M203-style grenade launcher, (AUG-8), muzzle cap, sling, cleaning kit and bipod with wire cutter and rifle grenades. The saw-backed bayonet, like those of AK, can be used as an insulated wire cutter and has a screwdriver in the scabbard.

The **AUG** is used by the Australian SAS, Moroccan Army, Netherlands Marines, New Zealand SAS, Oman Independant Reconnaissance Regiment, Saudi Arabian Army and Irish Rangers.

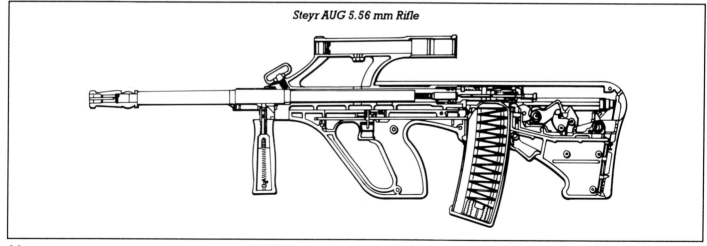

Steyr AUG 5.56 mm Rifle

Specification

Steyr AUG 5.56 mm Rifle

Cartridge: 5.56 mm x 45 mm
        M198 or NATO
Operating system: gas selective fire
Weight, empty: 3.85 kg
Length, overall: 790 mm
Barrel: 508 mm
Feed mechanism: 30 or 42-round box
magazine
Rate of fire: 650 rounds/min
Manufacturer: Steyr-Mannlicher GmbH,
Austria

An Austrian soldier lines up a target during covert operation training.

AK and AKS-74 5.45 mm Assault Rifles

The **AK-74** was introduced into service in the mid 1970s and saw action with the Soviet Army in the war in Afghanistan. The **AK-74** has a wooden butt, while the **AKS-74** has a tinny, folding metal butt; the AKSU-74 is a cut down sub-machine gun version which folds down to 490 mm, but fires the same powerful 5.45 mm round as the assault rifles using the same 30-round magazines.

The **AKS-74** is used by crews of armoured vehicles and Russian Spetznaz special forces. Like the AK-47 and AKM the mechanism of the **AK-74** is similar and therefore easy to use by reservists trained on these older weapons. The safety-catch and change-lever are on the right-hand side and from the 'Up safe' position move through a centre automatic setting to 'Down' for the single-shot position. Soviet doctrine was to fire on automatic. This approach to marksmanship, though less accurate than single shot, ensured that the enemy kept his head down under the heavy volume of fire. The distinctive feature of the assault rifles and Light Machine Gun (LMG) is the big muzzle brake which allows the weapon to be fired in bursts without muzzle climb. The gases are forced upwards and forwards which also prevents the blast coming back towards the firer. The muzzle brake does not reduce flash and the **AK-74** has a pronounced flash. Lateral blast can also cause aural damage to men on either side - a problem for recruits firing on a range.

The **AK-74** and **AKS-74** use ammunition which has several unusual features: it has a high rate of spin and therefore tumbles when it hits soft targets. This tendency to tumble is also ensured by the internal design of the bullet. The outside is made of steel with a cladding to reduce barrel wear; inside there is a 3 mm air gap in the nose, with a 3 mm lead slug. The base is made from a tapered steel core which sets back the centre of gravity. The AKSU-74 has been copied in former Yugoslavia but chambered for the 5.56 mm NATO round intended for the export market.

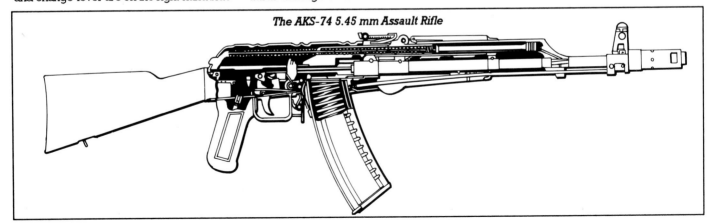

The AKS-74 5.45 mm Assault Rifle

Specification

AK-74 5.45 mm Assault Rifle

Cartridge: 5.45 mm x 39 mm
Operating system: Gas
Weight, empty: 3.6 kg
Length, overall: (AK-74) 930 mm
                    (AKS-74 690 mm
                    butt folded)
Barrel: 400 mm, 4 grooves rh
Feed mechanism: 30-round plastic box magazine
Rate of fire: 650 rpm cyclic
Muzzle velocity: 900 m/s
Manufacturer: State Industries

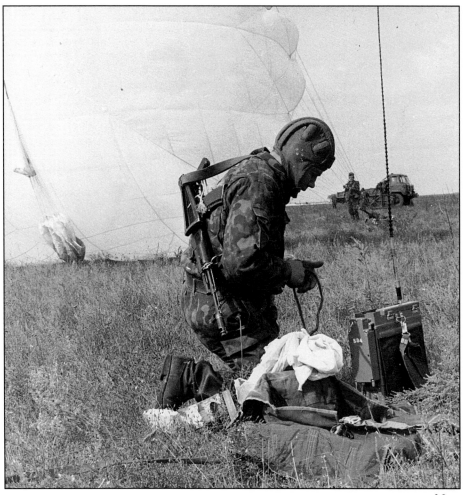

An AKS-74 carried by a member of the Russian Spetznaz special force during a training exercise.

The Accuracy International L96A1 Rifle   UK

During the 'Troubles' in Northern Ireland the Royal Marines used the Enfield L42A1 7.62 mm bolt action rifle which began life as the .303 in No 4 rifle. It was equipped with a new barrel, stripped down furniture and an L1A1 telescopic sight.

The **L96A1** which replaced the L42A1 uses the most modern materials. It has an aluminium frame to which the components are firmly attached. On the outside is a high impact green plastic stock in which the stainless steel barrel floats freely. The bolt-action is conventional with three forward lugs and a safety catch in the handle. Bolt lift is 60 degrees with a bolt throw of 107 mm. This allows the firer to stay in the aim while reloading.

The rifle has a light, fully-adjustable alloy bipod. The infantry version has adjustable iron sights out to 700 m, but is normally fitted with the Schmidt und Bender 6 x 42 telescopic sight, designated the L1A1. This gives a sniper the accuracy demanded by the British army of a first round hit at 600 m and harassing fire out to 1000 m.

The counter-terrorist version may be fitted with a 12 x or a 2.5 - 10 x as well as an infantry 6 x 42 sight. A spring-loaded monopod is stowed in the butt. This can be lowered and adjusted to support the weight of the rifle while the firer observes and lays on the target.

A suppressed rifle using sub-sonic ammunition is also produced, which is accurate out to 300 m without trajectory or wind deflection.

The rifle is produced in single-shot Magnum calibres for long-range anti-terrorist work and calibres are now .300 Winchester Magnum and 7 mm Remington Magnum for use up to 1000 m. An 8.6 mm cartridge is under development for ranges up to and exceeding 1000 m.

A 'Covert' sniper rifle consists of a suppressed Precision Magazine (PM) which can be taken down with the butt hinging forward and the barrel unscrewed to fit into an airline style case which also holds the sights and magazines.

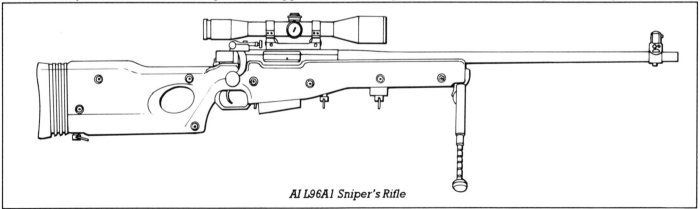

AI L96A1 Sniper's Rifle

Specification

Cartridge: 7.62 x 51 mm NATO
Operating system: bolt-action
Weight: 6.20 kg
Length: 1163 mm
Barrel: 655 mm
Feed: 10-round box magazine
Manufacturer: Accuracy International,
Portsmouth, UK

*A British Army sniper in his camouflaged
'ghillie suit' with an L96A1 rifle.*

MAG 7.62 mm Machine Gun   Belgium

The **FN Mitrailleuse à Gaz** or **MAG** is one of the most successful General Purpose Machine Guns (GPMGs) to be manufactured since the war. There are over 150,000 guns in service with more than 75 countries.

The **MAG** uses the feed mechanism developed by the Germans for the MG42 during World War II. This gives it a rate of fire of between 650 and 1000 rounds per minute. The rates of fire can be adjusted by opening or closing the gas regulator which controls the flow of gas from the barrel back onto the cupped piston-head. Gunners learn to 'balance' their weapon so that this gas flow gives an optimum performance.

The **MAG** can be used in the light role with a bipod or on a sustained fire (SF) spring buffered tripod. In the SF role a butt plate is fitted and the rear sight flips up and shows ranges between 800 and 1800 metres. An optical sight can also be fitted which allows the gun to be fired on pre-registered targets which may be obscured by darkness or smoke.

During fighting in Oman in the 1970s the SAS used the **MAG** in the SF role, because though the tripod was an extra weight, it ensured a stable mount which allowed the gun to fire accurately at distant targets. In the light role the sights lie flat and are graduated between 200 and 800 metres in 100 m intervals. The gun is easy to strip and clean in the field, with the piston and bolt assembly in one piece and the only small parts being the collets on the gas regulator.

With a butt plate fitted, the **MAG** is an ideal weapon for light vehicles. It can be installed on a pintle mount in front of the passenger seat; a second weapon can be fitted at the back of the vehicle, giving a total potential fire power of nearly 2000 rounds per minute.

Fitted to vehicles in this way the **MAG** was used by the SAS in the Gulf in 1991.

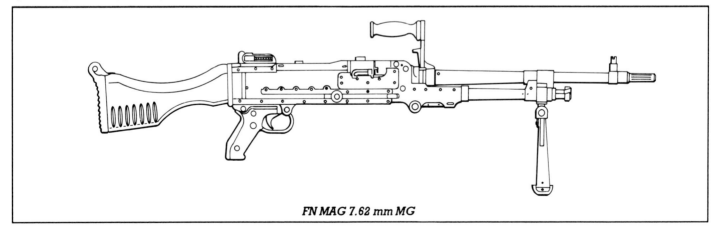

FN MAG 7.62 mm MG

Specification

Cartridge: 7.62 x 51 mm NATO
Operating system: Gas, automatic
Weight, empty: 11.65 kg.
(with butt and bipod)
Length, overall: 1260 mm
Barrel: 548 mm, 4 grooves, rh
Feed system: disintegrating link belt
Rate of Fire: 650 to 1000 rds/min (cyclic)
Muzzle velocity: 840 m/s
Manufacturer: FN Herstal Voie de Liège 33,
B-4040 Herstal, Belgium

An FN MAG GPMG being cleared by the gunner during a line firing exercise.

Minimi 5.56 mm Machine Gun   Belgium

Designed by The Belgian Fabrique Nationale (FN), **Minimi** is an ideal weapon for sustained fire since it can fire either belted disintegrating link SS 109 NATO or US M193 5.56 mm ammunition; it also interfaces well with the American M16 30-round box magazines and most NATO rifles. The feed is from the left.

A 200-round box of belted ammunition can be clipped directly to the **Minimi** which makes it a formidable close-quarter battle weapon. When a magazine is in place the belt feed will not function and vice-versa.

The **Minimi** is a gas-operated weapon which is normally fired from its bipod, although a sustained fire tripod is available. The gun handles like a baby brother of the FN 7.62 mm MAG. It has a top cover and the cocking handle is on the right, with a gas regulator which has two settings, normal and adverse. The latter setting ensures a sufficient flow of gas against the piston to clear a malfunction. The adjustment can be made even when the barrel is hot. The recoil force is less than that of a full size 7.62 mm round, and consequently it can be fired with greater accuracy. The **Minimi** can be fitted with a backplate for use in helicopters and vehicles where a butt would be a hindrance. The standard weapon has a 465 mm barrel, but a more compact Para model for airborne forces has a 347 mm barrel, which means that with the wire stock folded it is only 768 mm long.

The Para model at 7.1 kg is 0.15 kg heavier than the standard weapon, but its compact size means that it is ideal where heavy short-range fire is required, for example, in room clearing operations or anti-ambush drills.

The **Minimi** has been adopted by the Australians, the Belgian, Canadian, Indonesian, and Italian Armed forces where it is designated the F89. In US service it is known as the M249 Squad Automatic Weapon (SAW). It is in use with the British SAS. This widespread use means that it is not a signature weapon. It has been used in action by US forces in Panama, the Gulf and Somalia, and by Belgian and Australian forces in Rwanda.

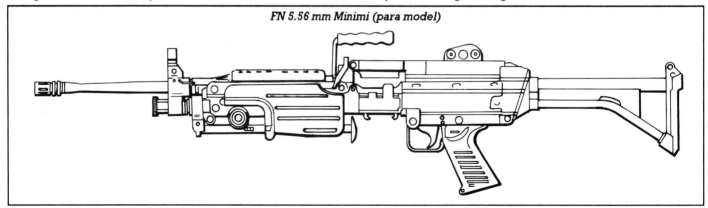

FN 5.56 mm Minimi (para model)

Specification

Cartridge: 5.56 x 45 mm (NATO)
Operating system: Gas
Weight, empty: 6.85 kg (standard)
7.1 kg (para)
Length, overall: 1040 mm (standard)
915 mm (para,stock extended)
768 mm (para, stock folded)
Barrel: 465 mm, 6 grooves, rh (standard)
347 mm (para)
Feed system: Disintegrating link belt or
M16-type box magazine
Rate of Fire: 700 to 1000 rounds per
minute (cyclic)
Muzzle velocity: 915 m/second (NATO)
965 m/sec (M193)
Manufacturer: FN Herstal, Voie de Liège 33,
B-4040 Herstal, Belgium

A British soldier aims his FN Minimi fitted with a Pilkington Optronics Kite night-sight.

The **PK** machine gun introduced into service with the Soviet Army in 1964 was widely exported in the 1970s and 80s. It uses the basic Kalashnikov action with a gas cylinder under the quick-change barrel. The modified feed system uses the strong ejection pull to load the belted full-size ammunition. When fired from vehicles or on a sustained fire mount it uses 50-round magazines or 250-round boxes.

The **PK** was followed by the **PKM,** an improved, slightly lighter model which was easier to manufacture. The **PK** and the **PKM** use a full size 7.62 x 54 round, which can engage targets out to 1000 metres, and has great penetration.

At close range the 7.62 x 54 round can cut through 37 mm of mild steel, 127 mm of concrete, 178 mm of sand and 280 mm of earth. At 50 metres a competent gunner has a 97% chance of hitting a man-sized moving target with a 6 to 9-round burst; at 100 metres it is 83%; at 175 metres 69% and at 250 metres 56%. At 1000 metres the chances sink to a mere 3%.

On a sustained fire tripod the **PKM** is designated the PKB and PKMB and at 1000 metres a gunner has a 50% chance of hitting a team-sized target with a 6 to 9-round burst.

At Fort Benning the US Army conducted extensive trials on weapons captured during the Vietnam War and though the **PK** had 100 metres less effective range than the M60 and a non-disintegrating ammunition belt it was reckoned to be superior to the M60 because it was lighter, more reliable and had a lower stoppage rate. For these reasons, and its availability from captured stocks, the **PK** was adopted by the Rhodesian SAS, the Selous Scouts and South African Special Forces like Koevoet, a police anti-terrorist unit which operated in Namibia. The **PK** is still in use in Afghanistan, the Middle East and former Soviet Central Asia, and it will thus be a favoured choice by Special Forces as a sterile weapon.

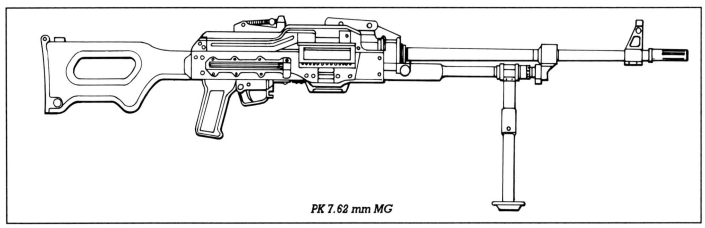

PK 7.62 mm MG

Specification

Cartridge: 7.62 x 54 R
Operating system: Gas, automatic
Weight, empty: 9.0 kg
Length, overall: 1160 mm
Barrel: 658 mm, 4 grooves, rh
Feed system: 100, 200 or 250-round belt
Rate of fire: 700 rounds/min (cyclic)
Muzzle velocity: 825 m/s
Manufacturer: CIS, State Arsenals

Captured PK machine guns collected by US forces following the invasion of Grenada in 1983.

M60 7.62 mm Machine Gun

The combat debut of the **M60** in Vietnam, as a vehicle and helicopter mounted weapon and infantry machine gun, was less than happy. The gun was nicknamed by some soldiers 'the Pig' for its tendency to jam and the fact that, with the bipod legs attached to the barrel, changing a hot barrel in a fire fight could be a complex operation. Unlike other gas operated weapons it did not have an adjustable regulator, so malfunctions, through build up of carbon after sustained firing, could not be resolved by closing up the gas regulator. However, since the 1960s these problems have been eradicated.

The current weapons retain an interesting feature from the original gun, in that they can be stripped using a live round as a tool. The **M60** has a slow cyclic rate which ensures that the gunner can stay in aim and fire accurately.

There are five versions of the **M60:** the standard LMG version; the M60D pintle-mounted gun used by door gunners in helicopters, on vehicles and small craft; the M60E2 fitted in armoured fighting vehicles (AFVs); and the M60E3, a lightweight model with a forward grip and a shorter (560 mm) barrel which has the bipod attached to the front of the receiver. This last version weighs 9.1 kg compared to the 11.1 kg of the **M60.** A conversion kit from the manufacturers allows the receiver of an **M60** to be converted to bring the gun to E3 standard.

M60s are in service with special forces of the US, Australia, South Korea, Taiwan and other national forces. This wide use makes it ideal for special forces since it is not a 'signature' weapon. For this specialised work day and night sights, and laser range finders, can be fitted without the weapon going out of zero.

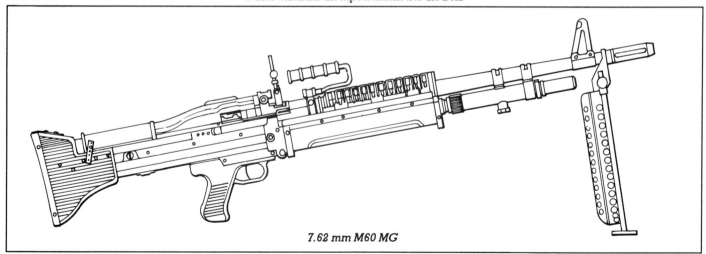

7.62 mm M60 MG

Specification

Cartridge: 7.62 x 51 mm NATO
Operating system: Gas
Weight, empty: 11.1 kg
Length, overall: 1105 mm
Barrel: 560 mm, 6 grooves, rh
Feed system: Disintegrating link belt
Rate of fire: 600-650 rounds/min
Muzzle velocity: 853 m/s
Manufacturer: Saco Defense, Saco, Maine

An Australian soldier armed with an M60 machine gun during exercises.

MP5/MPK Series Sub-machine Gun   Germany

When the SAS collaborated with GSG9, the German counter-terrorist team, at Mogadishu in 1977 they forged an excellent relationship with cross-training and equipment evaluation. One of the weapons that the SAS adopted was the German **Heckler & Koch MP 5** sub-machine gun.

The SAS team that cleared the Iranian Embassy at Princes Gate, London, in 1980, were armed with **MP5s** and since then it has become the preferred weapon for counter-terrorist operations. Close protection teams in Northern Ireland use the **MP5.**

The **MP5's** strengths include rapid firing, with a cyclic rate of 800 rounds per minute, whilst remaining accurate and completely reliable. This is achieved by the delayed blowback operation which is more reliable than conventional blowback-operated sub-machine guns.

The **MP5 Series** can be fitted with passive night sights, a x4 telescopic sight or a Henscholdt Aiming Point infra-red aiming marker.

The AMP5 2 is the standard weapon and has a fixed butt. The MP5 A3 has a folding metal strut stock with the MP5 A4 having a fixed butt and a three-round burst facility. The MP5 A5E has a fixed butt and automatic and three-round burst facilities which means that with its awesome cyclic rate of 900 rounds per minute it will exhaust a 15-round magazine in a second! The **MP5 SD** is a silenced model, produced in six versions that share the common feature of a two-part silencer, which reduces the velocity of the 9 mm x 19 Parabellum round, diverts the gases and muffles the exit report.

The MPK Series was introduced for use by special police and anti-terrorist squads. They are extra short and can be carried inside clothing, car glove-pockets or other restricted space. They are fitted with a prominent forehand grip which gives the firer the best control using all types of fire. They lack a butt-stock and are designed to be fired from a hand-hold without other supports. All models in the MPK Series offer the same fire options as the MP5 Series.

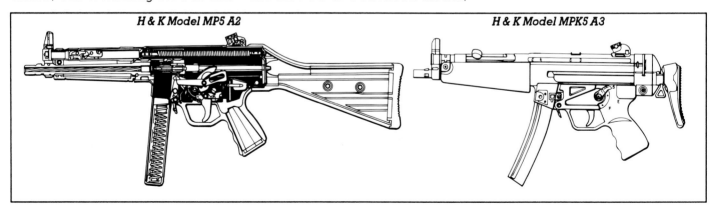

H & K Model MP5 A2   *H & K Model MPK5 A3*

Specification

MP5 Sub-machine Gun Series

Cartridge: 9 mm x 19 Parabellum
Operating system: delayed blowback, selective fire
Weight, empty: 2.55 kg
Length: 680 mm (fixed butt, MP5 A2)
490 mm (butt retracted, MP5 A3)
Barrel: 225 mm
Feed: 15 or 30-round box magazine
Muzzle velocity: 400 m/s
Rate of Fire: 800 rds/min (cyclic)
Manufacturer: Heckler & Koch GmbH, Oberndorf-Neckar, Germany

MPK5 Sub-machine Gun Series

As above, but:
Weight, empy: 2 kg
Length: 325 mm
Barrel: 115 mm
Rate of Fire: 900 rds/min (cyclic)

A Royal Green Jacket officer fires the MP5A3 on a range in the UK.

Small Arms

Though Special Forces may use silenced rifles and pistols and other unusual weapons for their work, they often favour existing widely-used weapons because their appearance does not attract attention. Reliable captured weapons, with their registered number removed, can be used as 'sterile' small arms which cannot be traced if captured.

The capacity for automatic pistols to hold ten, or more, rounds makes them the obvious choice in preference to revolvers. Dating from the 1920s, the Browning 9 mm High Power pistol was the first weapon designed with a large capacity magazine. It was used by the SAS in World War II and still a favourite part of their armoury.

The adoption of 5.56 mm as the calibre for the M16 assault rifle, used by the US Army in the Vietnam War, led to its being chosen to supersede the larger, heavier 7.62 mm calibre. Using the 5.56 mm ammunition the M16 suffered from teething troubles when it was introduced, but the Austrian Steyr AUG, after careful research with the same 5.56 mm ammunition, has proved a reliable weapon widely favoured by regular and Special Forces alike. A veteran of SAS operations in Oman recalled that he was glad that he was carrying the lighter, smaller calibre ammunition for his improved M16.

The former Soviet Union, with the 7.62 mm AK47, had been a small arms pioneer: but, seeing merit in smaller calibre ammunition, chose an even smaller 5.45 mm calibre.

In a fire-fight, normally at quite short ranges, it was the volume of fire that counted, not the calibre. During the Vietnam War, Eugene Stoner, the designer of the M16, produced the Stoner System: a 'family' of weapons which had interchangeable parts between the LMG and rifle; but, although Stoner weapons were trialled by SEALS, they were not adopted; however, the 'family' approach to small-arms design gained favour because, in the field, damaged weapons parts could be interchangeable if spares were not available from stores; also, spares inventories could be kept small. The Austrian Steyr AUG is a good example of a weapons family. The former Soviet Union has also produced weapons, in 7.62 mm and 5.45 mm, which include assault rifles and light machine guns with interchangeable parts.

The M203, which combines a 5.56 mm assault rifle with a 40 mm grenade launcher, has been widely adopted and copied. It gives both direct and indirect fire capability in one weapon and is the pointer to future personal weapons design.

For the longer ranges, at which a machine-gunner might be required to engage targets, the full size 7.62 mm is still favoured. The American M60, the Belgian FN MAG and the CIS PK/PKM series GPMGs allow patrols to reach out to ranges over 1000 metres; the bigger round is also used by snipers. The volume of fire from a belt-fed weapon creates a 'beaten zone' which effectively denies ground to an unprotected enemy. All of these machine-guns are in widespread use and therefore are ideal for Special Forces.

The Browning .50 in is the grandfather of all these weapons, tracing its origins back to a requirement for a heavy machine gun issued by the US Army at the end of World War I. The ammunition is based on German anti-tank rifle rounds captured in 1918. Despite this vintage the '50 cal' is a rugged and reliable weapon which has been used in all the major conflicts from World War II to Bosnia. Over the years it has been modified in a few areas, including a quick change barrel, but the basic gun will probably see the century out mounted on Special Forces vehicles.

Support Weapons

Special Forces, in action, are always in need of the firepower of support weapons. These are the weapons giving heavier support than small arms, but not so heavy as artillery or airborne weapon support.

The belt-fed American Mk 19 Mod 3 40 mm automatic grenade launcher has been copied by several countries. This was shown in a film of Soviet Spetznaz troops in Afghanistan, deploying from a Mil Mi-8 'Hip' helicopter, positioning the very similar AGS-17 30 mm 'Plamya' grenade launcher. Belt-fed grenade launchers can put down a heavy volume of direct fire or can lob rounds over cover. They are light enough to be fitted to Special Forces vehicles such as Land Rovers or HMMWVs (see separate entry).

The 66 mm Light Anti-armour Weapon (LAW) is a weapon which grew out of the Vietnam War. It is a one-shot, recoilless anti-tank weapon which can be discarded after use, or it can be used as shown in the Adder/Arges entry, as an anti-tank mine for setting up ambushes.

As tank armour has increased, the required calibre of these weapons has necessarily increased also. The US Army adopted the 84 mm AT-4 anti-tank weapon, manufactured by Bofors Ordnance of Sweden, as a replacement for the LAW. It was used in action by US Rangers in the assault on Panama City in Operation 'Just Cause' in 1989.

Anti-tank weapons have, of course, been used against hostile armour, but are more commonly used against enemy bunkers. Bofors Ordnance have produced ammunition types fitted with fuzes which can be set to penetrate bunker walls before they explode.

The British L16 81 mm mortar is widely used around the world and was employed in action by the SAS in Oman and the Falkland Islands. This medium-calibre mortar gives firepower to over six kilometres, which is ideal for diversionary and deceptive plans which Special Forces may be required to use as part of a larger operation.

If the enemy locate a Special Forces patrol they may engage them with armour or aircraft. The Milan and Stinger anti-tank and anti-aircraft missiles will not hold off a determined attack by large numbers of these vehicles or aircraft, but they will serve as a very effective deterrent to an unsupported enemy.

Stinger can be used aggressively by patrols waiting in ambush to attack airfields. Soviet forces in Afghanistan were plagued by Mujihadeen rebels using Stingers against fixed wing aircraft and helicopters; this forced the Mil Mi-24 'Hind' attack helicopters to fly higher so that their attacks became less accurate.

As with other anti-tank weapons the Milan has been updated and enhanced since its introduction. New warheads, guidance and night-sights have given the Milan anti-tank guided-missiles (ATGM) a day and night capability as well as the power to penetrate the armour of most Armoured Fighting Vehicles (AFV). Similarly, Special Forces have used ATGM against enemy positions and bunkers using the AT-4.

The 30 mm ASP (see separate entry) gives Special Forces a very useful weapon for stand-off attacks against industrial targets which may be vulnerable to 'surgical' hits against individual valves, conduits, control mechanisms and the like, or simply as a support weapon giving hefty back-up fire-power.

Browning .50 in. M2HB Machine Gun USA

The Browning 'Big Fifty' is one of the longest serving weapons in the special forces armoury. It entered service with the US Army in 1923 and it was used in World War II by SAS patrols in North Africa who mounted it on their Jeeps. The SAS were still using it over 50 years later in Iraq during the Gulf War of 1990-91, where troopers noted that some of the guns were a great deal older than their users!

The sights are graduated up to 2600 yards (2378 metres) but the big rounds are effective beyond this range. The ammunition was developed from German anti-tank rifle rounds captured at the end of World War I and is effective against lightly armoured vehicles. A French-made armour-piercing ammunition weighs 47.82 g and will penetrate 25 mm of steel at 300 m and 13 mm at 1200 m. Among the natures available are ball, tracer, incendiary and armour-piercing incendiary. This has allowed gunners to mix and match linked ammunition so that it is most effective against likely targets.

The gun has been mounted in aircraft, aboard ships of all displacements, from battleships to river patrol craft, on armoured and soft skinned vehicles and on a tripod in the ground role; with infantry using high-angle anti-aircraft mounts and buffered systems. A selectable slow cyclic rate of 450-600 rounds per minute is available to improve accuracy.

Improvements on this battle-tested design include the RAMO and Saco .50 M2HB quick-change kit and the M2 lightweight machine gun, which weighs 26.72 kg compared to the 38 kg of the **M2HB**. The rate of fire on the lightweight gun can be adjusted between 550 and 750 rounds per minute to allow the weapon to be used in ground support or air defence roles. The quick-change kits not only allow hot barrels to be changed quickly and safely after prolonged firing, but also eliminate the time consuming task of headspace adjustment.

The **Browning M2HB .50** is an ideal weapon for vehicle mounted special forces operations because of its range and destructive power and also because it is widely used by over 30 countries and is therefore definitely not a signature weapon.

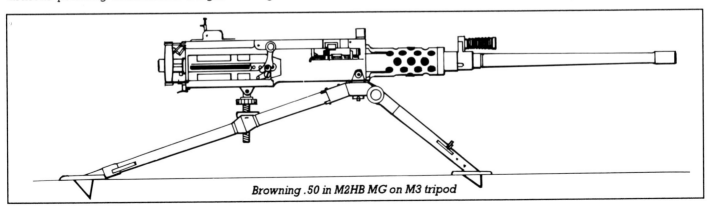

Browning .50 in M2HB MG on M3 tripod

Specification

Cartridge: .50 Browning (12.7 x 99 mm)
Operating system: Short recoil
Weight, empty: 38.15 kg
Length, overall: 1656 mm
Barrel: 1143 mm, 8 grooves, rh
Feed system: Disintegrating link belt
Rate of fire: 485 to 635 rounds/min
Muzzle velocity: 916 m/sec
Manufacturers: Ramo Manufacturing,inc.,
Nashville,TN,USA
Saco Defense inc.,
Saco,ME,USA
FN Herstal, Belgium

A Browning 'Big Fifty' M2HB heavy machine gun mounted on an M1 Abrams tank.

The Browning M2HB heavy machine gun fitted with a Multi-purpose Universal Gunner Sight.

M203 Grenade Launcher   USA

The Colt **M203 40 mm grenade launcher**, which replaced the M79 during the Vietnam War, fits underneath an assault rifle, usually the M16. The barrel, trigger mechanism, sights and hand-guard can be fitted quickly to a standard weapon without the use of special tools. The quadrant sight is on the left side of the rifle and is adjustable in 25 metre increments up to 400 metres, whilst a leaf-sight, on the receiver, is adjustable up to 250 metres in 50 metre increments.

To load the **M203**, the grenadier slides the barrel forward and inserts a round; this has the advantage of allowing him to operate the weapon in a prone position during a fire fight. A loaded M16A1 rifle fitted with the **M203** launcher weighs 5.484 kg.

The 40 mm round fired from an **M203** can hit area targets out to 350 metres and point targets to 150 metres.

Ammunition natures include: M406 HE; M647 CS; M433 Fragmentation Shaped Charge; M576E1 (a 20-ball shotgun round); green, red, and yellow smoke and green and red para illumination rounds. The HE, which is gold coloured, has an effective casualty radius of five metres.

With practice a 40 mm round can be fired through a window at 150 metres and this accuracy compensates for the modest lethality of the weapon.

The rounds produce a low recoil when fired and have a muzzle velocity of 76 m/s.

It is in use with armies whose infantry are equipped with M16 rifles, and therefore the **M203** is not a signature weapon. It has become widely favoured by British, United States and Israeli special forces and has seen action in all of the land conflicts fought by the United States since the 1970s.

The **M203** allows 5.56 mm rifle fire on to observed targets, whilst the 40 mm grenades can be lobbed into dead ground.

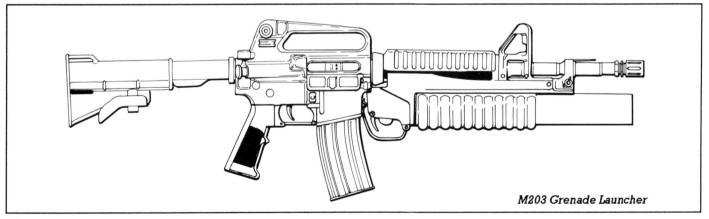

M203 Grenade Launcher

Specifications :

Projectile: 40 mm grenade
Operation: single shot
Weight in firing order: 1.63 kg
Length: 380 mm
Feed: breech loading, sliding barrel
Maximum range: 400 m
Muzzle velocity: 75 m/s with M406 grenade
Rate of fire: 6 to 8 rounds per minute
Manufacturer: Colt's Manufacturing Co Inc, USA

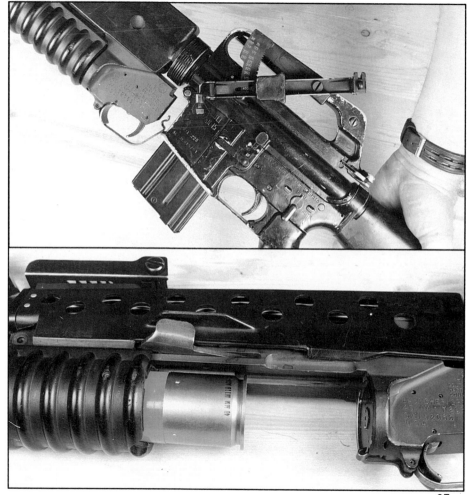

Detailed pictures of the M203 launcher showing the loading mechanism and sights.

Mk 19 Mod 3 40 mm Grenade Launcher USA

From the M79 40 mm 'Blooper' in Vietnam the obvious move was to develop an automatic grenade launcher which could be mounted on helicopters, small boats or vehicles. The US Navy, which had been operating a 'Brown Water Fleet' in small patrol boats in the Mekong Delta, was the driving force in the development programme. The **Mk 19** which resulted is an air-cooled, blowback type, automatic machine gun which fires a variety of 40 mm grenades with a muzzle velocity of 241 metres per second. The ammunition has a unique link which stays with the cartridge case and is ejected with the case after firing. The gun is fired from an open bolt position with the ammunition feed operating during recoil similar to the M2 machine gun. The **Mk 19** can be fired manually or remotely using an electrical solenoid, a single round at a time or on full automatic at 325 to 375 rounds per minute. This rate of fire and the ammunition, M430 HE dual purpose AP and armour piercing round, make the **Mk19** an awesome weapon. Ammunition is stowed in 20 or 50-round containers; this concept is copied by several countries including the former Soviet Union with the 30 mm AGS-17 and Singapore's CIS 40-AGL.

The US Naval Ordnance Station, Louisville, Kentucky which had developed the **Mk 19** worked on the design and by the late 1970s had produced the Mod 3 which had 47% fewer working parts and could be stripped without using special tools.

The **Mk 19 Mod 3** has five major sub-assemblies: the bolt, backplate, sear, top cover, feed-slide and tray, and receiver. In the ground role it is mounted on Mk 64 Mod 4 Mount. The sights, spade grips and charger assembly are similar to those of the Browning M2 .50 in machine gun.

The **Mk 19** was mounted on HMMWVs and Fast Attack Vehicles used by US Special Forces in the Gulf in 1991. It has an effective range of 1500 metres and this combined with its steady rate of fire makes it highly effective, complementing longer range weapons like the Browning .50 in machine gun.

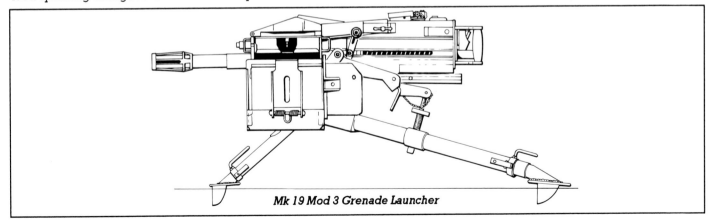

Mk 19 Mod 3 Grenade Launcher

Specification

Projectile: 40 mm M385, M385E4, M430 and M918 grenades
Operating system: Blowback
Weight, empty: 35.3 kg
Length, overall: 1095 mm
Feed system: Disintegrating link belt
Rate of fire: 325 to 375 rounds/min
Muzzle velocity: 241 m/sec
Effective range: 1,500 m
Manufacturer: Saco Defense Inc, USA

The 40mm Mk 19 on a ground mount fitted with a laser range finder.

Milan Anti-tank Guided Weapon   France

The **Milan** medium-range anti-tank guided weapon (ATGW), developed by Euromissile, a consortium of Aerospatiale of France, Deutsche Aerospace of Germany and British Aerospace, is one of the most successful missiles in its class. It is a wire guided SACLOS (Semi Automatic Command Line of Sight) missile ; the gunner need only keep the cross hairs on the target and the guidance information is automatically passed to the missile. At launch it moves at 75 m/s and then accelerates to 200 m/s, taking about 12.5 seconds to travel up to 2000 metres. The missile consists of a two-stage solid-fuel rocket with a shaped charge warhead. At launch it is projected from the tube by a gas generator, which also ejects the tube to the rear. The guidance system consists of a gas-driven turbine-operated gyro, an infra-red flare, a spool carrying the two guidance wires in one cable, a decoder unit, and a self-activating battery for internal power supply.

Externally Milan does not appear to have changed greatly from the original firing post and missile in its launch tube. One significant change is the MIRA thermal imaging sight which has been fitted above the firing post and allows the missile to be used by day or night. However, within the missile tube the weapon has changed considerably.

In 1984 **Milan 2** was introduced, with the warhead diameter increased from 103 mm to 115 mm and the explosive weight from 1.2 kg to 1.8 kg. The most striking feature was the probe which added 145 mm to the length of the warhead, but which gave an improved effect to the shaped charge by increasing the stand off.

In trials, **Milan 2** penetrated 1060 mm of armour. The **Milan 2** can be fired from existing firing posts. **Milan 2T** uses a tandem warhead which will penetrate explosive reactive armour (ERA). The probe contains the primary charge which disrupts the ERA and then the main warhead explodes. **Milan 3** has a flashing Xenon lamp in the tail, replacing the infra-red flare which was tracked by the guidance system and which could be 'spoofed' by flares.

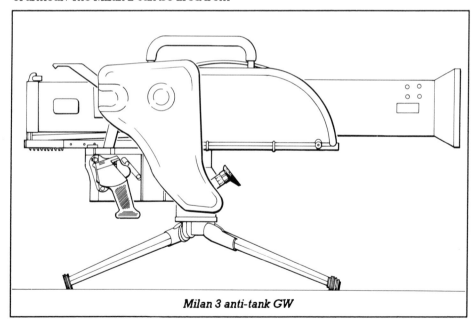

Milan 3 anti-tank GW

Specification

Guidance: Semi-automatic, wire
Warhead diameter: 133 mm
Warhead weight: 3.12 kg
Firing post weight: 16.9 kg
Missile weight: 11.91 kg
Missile length: 1200 mm
Max. effective range: 2000 m
Max. velocity: 210 m/s
Penetration of armour: >1000 mm
Manufacturer: Aerospatiale-Missiles, France

A Milan fitted with Pilkington Optronics thermal imaging sight in use with special forces.

The **Automatic Self Powered (ASP) 30 mm cannon** was developed by McDonnell Douglas as a combat support weapon that could be used in the same role as the Browning .50 heavy machine gun.

The **ASP** cannon has built-in dual recoil adapters which damp the recoil forces allowing it to be mounted on the Browning M2HB tripod or vehicles fitted with a compatible turret ring. **ASP** is a gas -operated weapon using a rotating bolt to lock the breech securely during the firing phase. The feed is single, from the left side, and the short length of the receiver behind the feed allows simple and easy control via spade-grips from inside the cupola of a vehicle.

The attraction of the **ASP** is that it fires standard ADEN/DEFA M789 pattern 30 mm ammunition which is used in a wide range of combat aircraft, so re-supply is not a problem. Among the manufacturers of this nature of ammunition are GIAT and Manhurin in France, Armscor in South Africa, FN in Belgium, Bofors in Sweden, Honeywell in the USA and Royal Ordnance in the UK.

The ammunition includes high explosive (HE), armour-piercing (AP), dual purpose HE, anti-tank with a fragmentation effect, HE incendiary as well as inert training rounds. The ammunition is particularly powerful with muzzle velocities of 600 to 820 metres per second. It is also larger than any heavy machine-gun ammunition - the heaviest Browning .50 is the Chinese NORINCO AP Incendiary which weighs 48.2 grams, while the GIAT AP Type 5970 and Manhurin HE/I F 5270 30 mm ammunition weigh 275 grams.

The **ASP** can be fitted with a range of night vision equipment including thermal imaging (TI) and image intensifying (II) as well as a laser range finder.

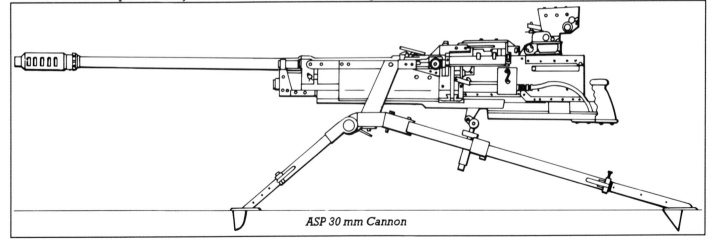

ASP 30 mm Cannon

Specification

Cartridge: 30 x 113B ADEN/DEFA
Operating system: Gas, automatic
Weight, empty: 52 kg
Length, overall: 2060 mm
Barrel: 1321 mm
Feed system: Disintegrating link belt
Rate of Fire: 450 rounds/min
Muzzle velocity: 820 m/s
Manufacturer: McDonnell Douglas, USA

British soldiers with an ASP in its ground role on a Browning M2HB tripod.

AT4 Anti-tank Launcher   Sweden

The Germans pioneered the one-shot anti-tank weapon in the latter years of World War II, but it was in the 1960s that the United States, with the 66 mm Light Anti-tank Weapon (LAW), produced a benchmark weapon. Subsequent designs have retained the telescopic design of the LAW or fitted an anti-tank rocket into a 1 metre tube.

The LAW design has been copied by the countries of the former Warsaw Pact and Soviet Union even down to the illustrated instructions on the barrel.

All infantry anti-tank weapons have shaped-charge warheads. Shaped charges are made from a cone-shaped explosive charge which has a copper or metal lining. When the charge explodes, initiated from the back of the cone, the cone collapses and focuses the energy into a small area as well as turning the copper into a slug (or self forging fragment) which rides on a stream of explosive gas or plasma. This energy will punch through armour and enter the tank or AFV. The slug ricochets around the interior of the vehicle, while the gas ignites fuel and ammunition.

To replace the LAW the US Army has adopted the Swedish 84 mm **AT4,** a non-telescopic weapon which weighs 6.7 kg, is 1000 mm long, has an effective range of 300 metres and can penetrate over 400 mm of armour. The **AT4** has also been produced as a Light Multi-purpose Assault Weapon (LMAW) for fighting in built up areas. It fires a round developed from the 84 mm HEDP Carl Gustav system. It can be set for 'D'- Delay or 'I' - Instantaneous. The 'I' mode is for use against AFVs where it causes considerable behind-armour damage. In 'D' mode the round penetrates bunkers or buildings before it explodes which means that over-pressure kills or injures the occupants.

The AT4CS which is under development can be fired in a confined space, which allows the weapon to be used in buildings.

AT12-T is a 120 mm weapon, similar in design and operation to the **AT 4**. It has a range of over 300 metres and can penetrate over 950 mm of armour. A folding mount allows the weapon to be fired from the prone, kneeling or standing position. It has a tandem warhead which means that it can defeat ERA.

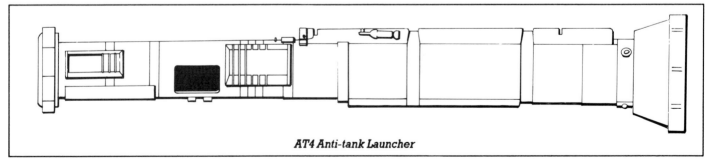

AT4 Anti-tank Launcher

Specification

AT-4 anti-tank weapon

Calibre of warhead: 84 mm
Weight, in firing order: 6.7 kg
Length of launcher: 1000 mm
Maximum range: 300 m
Maximum velocity: 290 m/sec
Penetration of Armour: >400 mm
Manufacturer: Bofors Ordnance, Sweden

In training with the AT-4 anti-tank weapon.

The larger calibre, 120 mm, AT12-T anti-tank weapon which weighs 14 kg and is 1.2 metres long.

Adder/Arges Anti-tank Mines International

Adder provides a low cost and simple method of firing LAW94, the British Army 94 mm one-shot anti-tank weapon. **Arges** is more sophisticated but both give Special Forces a potent ambush weapon against tanks and Armoured Personnel Carriers (APC).

The basic LAW94 is a 9 kg shoulder-fired weapon which is telescopic and can be expanded from 1 m to 1.5 m for firing. It has a powerful shaped charge which will penetrate 700 mm of armour. In its shoulder-fired role the soldier uses a ballistically matched spotting rifle to engage the target with tracer rounds; when they hit the tank or APC, he can fire the LAW.

Adder consists of a LAW94 mounted on a lightweight tripod with a firing unit, interconnecting cable, exploder and field packaging. When **Adder** has been set up to cover a road junction or defile, the soldier can withdraw and take cover. The mine is effective between 20 and 150 metres and, like the M18A1, is command detonated making it an ideal weapon for ambushes.

Arges, which weighs 18 kg and is 1.02 metres long, is a second generation off-route mine developed from LAW94 technology. It has a suite of sensors including IR with a ranging device and acoustic alerter. **Arges** brings together Hunting in the UK, Dynamit Nobel and Honeywell Regelsysteme from Germany and Giat Industries from France. One trained man can deploy **Arges** in less than five minutes in daylight. The **Arges** sensors can discriminate between target types and even let two vehicles pass before it fires. When the target is at its most vulnerable, the **Arges** sensor fires with a hit probability of 97% at 90 metres. The weapon has a tandem warhead which means that it will penetrate Explosive Reactive Armour. **Arges** can be programmed to be effective from three hours up to 40 days.

While **Adder** is part of a manned ambush, **Arges** could be left in place as a remote ambush to cover a withdrawal by Special Forces and linked into sensors like Classic.

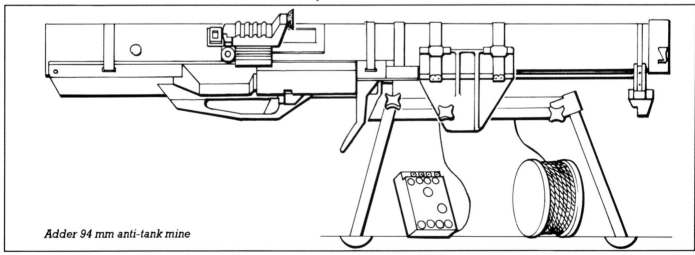

Adder 94 mm anti-tank mine

Specification

Adder Anti-tank Weapon

Calibre of warhead: 94 mm
Weight: 5.7 kg
Length: 610 mm
Width: 255 mm
Height: 460 mm
Effective range: 20 to 150 m
Warhead penetration: 700 mm
Manufacturer: Hunting Engineering UK;
Dynamit Nobel, Sweden;
Honeywell Regelsysteme, Germany;
GIAT Industries, France

The Addermine remote off-route anti-tank mine in position by a track. In an ambush it would be camouflaged and invisible to tank or AFV crews.

M18A1 Claymore Anti-personnel Mine   USA

The **M18A1 Claymore mine** was developed after the Korean War, when United Nations forces were confronted with massed assaults by Chinese infantry, who overwhelmed positions simply by their huge numbers.

Since its introduction in the 1960s the design has been copied widely. It consists of a curved plastic container with 700 steel spheres in a plastic matrix, behind which is a sheet of 682 g Composition C4 plastic explosive. The container stands on two sets of folding legs and has a simple peep-sight in the top as well as two fuze wells for the M4 blasting cap.

As with many items of US military equipment the **M18A1 Claymore** is issued with a set of illustrated instructions. These are in the M7 bandoleer which also contains 30 metres of brown cable, an M57 firing device commonly known as a 'Claymore clacker' and an M40 test set.

When a **Claymore** is fired the C4 explodes and blasts the 700 spheres in a fan shaped sheaf - these are lethal up to a height of two metres and to a range of 50 metres, though the danger area is almost 150 metres. There is a back-blast danger area of 16 metres; so, either the soldier firing the mine should be in cover, or, the mine should be sited with a bank behind it.

To set up a **Claymore** a soldier first identifies his 'killing zone'. He tests his M57 and then sites the mine using the peep-sight. He unrolls the cable and ties it to a secure object close to the mine so that animal or human movement will not tug it over. The detonator is inserted last, while the soldier has the M57 device with him, and then he takes up his ambush position, plugging in the cable to the firing device. The **Claymore** may be sited at ground level, but it can also be fixed into trees and even used in street fighting like a 'pole charge'.

M18A1 Claymore mines are used by both US and UK special forces and other NATO special units.

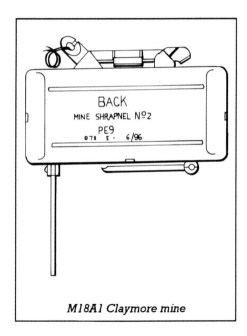

M18A1 Claymore mine

Specifications:

Weight: 1.58 g
Length: 216 mm
Width: 35 mm
Height: 83 mm
Lethal range: 50 metres
Manufacturer: Morton Thiokol Inc.,
Louisiana, USA

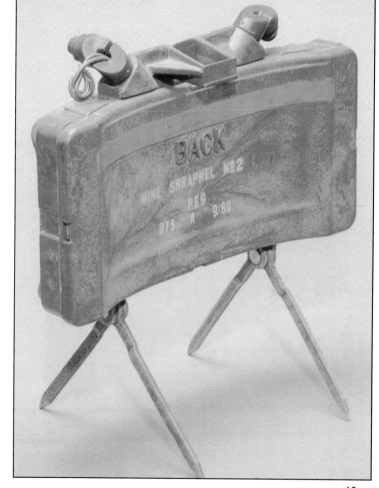

The South African version of the Claymore mine, the shrapnel Mine No. 2.

FIM-92 Stinger

The **Stinger** was first used in action by 22 SAS during the Falklands campaign of 1982; they shot down an Argentine Pucara ground attack aircraft, using an FIM-92A. Since then, in Mujihadeen hands, it has seen extensive action in Afghanistan against Soviet helicopters and fixed wing aircraft. It has been used in Nicaragua by the Contras and with UNITA in Angola.

Advocates of the missile say that at 15.7 kg it is an ideal weapon for Special Forces since, unlike other missiles which are meant to be man portable, it can be carried over long distances. In engagement, the operator receives audible signals as the infra-red seeker locks onto the enemy aircraft. The missile has a two stage motor; the first ejects the **Stinger** from its launch tube, but burns out before leaving the launch tube. This protects the gunner from blast injury. As it exits the tube the two movable and two fixed spring-loaded control surfaces deploy. After a few seconds, the second motor ignites and the Magnavox M934E6 fuzing circuit arms. Stinger is equipped with an Identification Friend or Foe (IFF) system which interrogates aircraft and reduces the danger of friendly fire. A self-destruct mechanism operates if the target is missed.

The **Stinger** has been upgraded and improved. The latest system, the FIM-92B/C, has an IR/UV guidance system which defeats IR flares fired by aircraft to 'spoof' the IR seeker head. **Stinger** has been fitted with a third generation image intensifying sight, which allows the operator to track and engage enemy aircraft and helicopters at night.

Stingers are used by the Israeli Parachute Corps, including the Sayeret reconnaissance units, and the Italian Folgore Airborne Brigade, the San Marco Marines and The Netherlands Marine Corps.

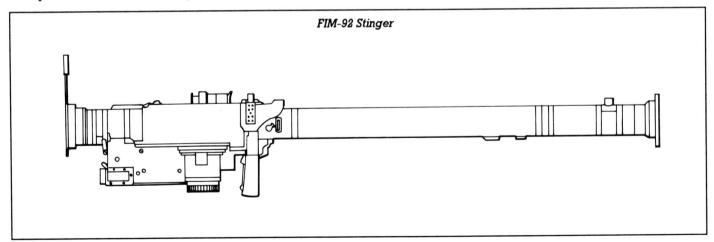

FIM-92 Stinger

Specifications:

Guidance: Infra-red homing
Warhead diameter: 70 mm
Warhead weight: 3 kg
Launch unit weight: 15.7 kg
Missile weight: 10.1 kg
Missile length: 1524 mm
Max effective range: >4500 m
Max. velocity: Mach 2.2
Manufacturer: General Dynamics, USA

A German soldier with Stinger ready for launch. The Identification Friend or Foe (IFF) antenna can be seen deployed forward of the sight.

L16 81mm Mortar

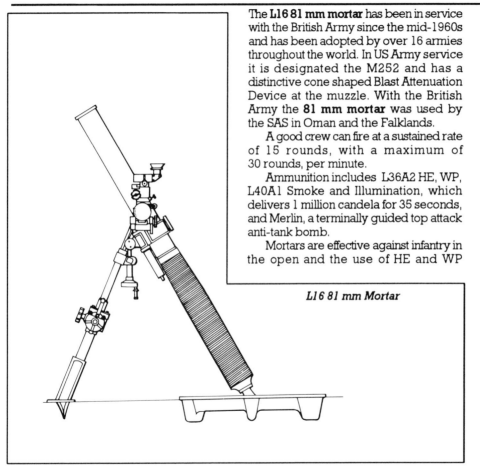

L16 81 mm Mortar

The **L16 81 mm mortar** has been in service with the British Army since the mid-1960s and has been adopted by over 16 armies throughout the world. In US Army service it is designated the M252 and has a distinctive cone shaped Blast Attenuation Device at the muzzle. With the British Army the **81 mm mortar** was used by the SAS in Oman and the Falklands.

A good crew can fire at a sustained rate of 15 rounds, with a maximum of 30 rounds, per minute.

Ammunition includes L36A2 HE, WP, L40A1 Smoke and Illumination, which delivers 1 million candela for 35 seconds, and Merlin, a terminally guided top attack anti-tank bomb.

Mortars are effective against infantry in the open and the use of HE and WP ammunition will neutralise an enemy position prior to an infantry assault and will blind armour by forcing it to close down.

The range span allows special forces to stand off from a large vulnerable target and deliver disruptive fire. In the Falklands, special forces used mortar fire in a number of deception operations to distract the Argentine garrison which occupied the islands.

Alhough the mortar is not light it can be broken down into loads that can be manpacked, enabling the crew to carry the mortar to remote locations. The barrel weighs 12.7 kg, the mounting 12.3 kg, the baseplate 11.6 kg and the sights 1.25 kg, The mortar can also be broken down and loaded into a 1/4 tonne vehicle and this allows the crew to come into and out of action very quickly - essential if they are engaging an enemy equipped with mortar-locating radar.

The sight is the Canadian C2 which is also used in the GPMG in its Special Forces role and is illuminated with a Tritium light source for night firing.

Hand held fire control computers on the mortar line allow target information to be stored and accessed quickly and Mortar Fire Controllers (MFC) with laser range finders and GPS (see entry) can pass very detailed target information back to the line.

Specification

Calibre: 81 mm
Elevation: 45 degrees to 80 degrees
Traverse: 7 degrees r and l on the bipod
Weight in firing position: 37.85 kg inc sight
Ammunition weight: 4.5 kg (approx.)
Maximum Range: 5650 m
Minimum Range: 100 m
Maximum muzzle velocity: 297 m/s
Rate of fire: 15 rounds/min
Manufacturer: Royal Ordnance UK

Soldiers of the Queen's Regiment train with an L16 81 mm mortar.

Irritant CS Smoke Grenade

O-chlorobenzlidene malonitrile (CS) is a clear white solid chemical. If burnt it produces a colourless gas with an acrid pepper like smell which is immediately irritating to the eyes and upper respiratory tract. In heavy concentrations CS may create nausea resulting in vomiting. Nausea and the illusion of suffocation typically cause the feeling of dizziness or 'swimming' sensation, so victims unused to tear gas commonly appear highly disorientated. The vapours created by the action of a burning agent mix with human sweat to cause a burning sensation to the skin. Especially affected are the areas of the face around the eyes, nose and mouth and the tender areas about the elbows, knees, crotch and buttocks. The full effects of CS vapours occur within 20 to 60 seconds after exposure. This will endure for up to ten minutes after escape from the vapour, with the possibility of skin rash persisting a day or so after heavy exposure. CS in powder form is initially not as fast-acting as vapour, however once it has gone into solution mixed with sweat and mucous the effect is similar to vapour.

CS gas was developed by the British at Porton Down (Wiltshire, UK) and was first used in action by British forces against rioters in Cyprus in the summer of 1958.

A CS grenade may be similar to a coloured smoke grenade, with an extruded aluminium casing and pin and fly-off handle. To operate, the pin is pulled and the handle held down until the moment that the grenade is thrown. After a delay of two to three seconds the burning CS vents from the bottom of the grenade for about 25 seconds.

Rubber-bodied grenades are designed to rupture and scatter burning pellets over a wide area. This ensures that the gas is effectively dispersed, and prevents the grenade from being thrown back.

CS gas, with stun grenades, have been used by special forces effecting entries in hostage rescue operations.

Within NATO, practice CS grenades are grey with a red hazard band.

The **N201 No.83 Irritant CS Smoke Grenade** is compact and extremely efficient where CS, in a smoke form, is required for dispersion in large open areas. It is used by the British SAS.

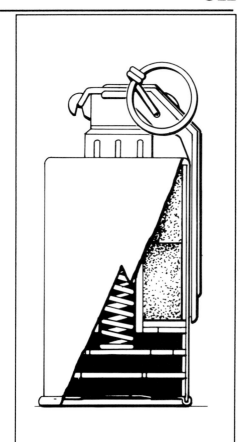

N201 No. 83 Irritant CS Smoke Grenade

Specification

Haley & Weller N201

Length: 135 mm
Diameter: 63 mm
Weight: 340 g
Nett explosive quantity: 205 g
Burn time: 25 seconds
Shelf life: 3 years
Manufacturer: Haley & Weller, Draycot, Derbyshire, UK

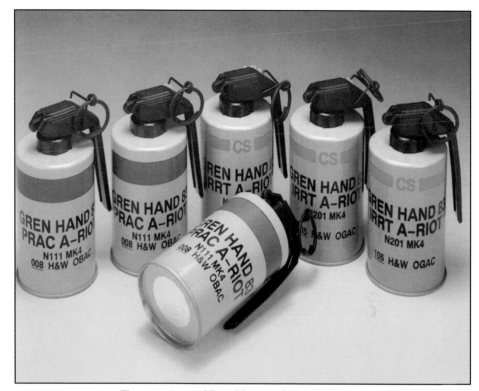

The practice and live CS grenades manufactured by Haley & Weller.

Stun grenades were developed in the United Kingdom to a requirement from the SAS. They were first used operationally at Mogadishu on 16th October 1977 when Major Alastair Morrison and Sergeant Barry Davies, of the SAS, assisted the men of GSG9, the German counter-terrorist force. A Lufthansa Boeing 737 had been hijacked by four Palestinian terrorists and flown to Mogadishu. As GSG9 assaulted the aircraft, stun grenades were thrown onto the wings to produce flashes and loud bangs to disorientate the hijackers.

Stun grenades, along with CS, were thrown into the Iranian Embassy by the SAS when they cleared it in May 1980.

Designs vary, but most stun grenades consist of a small lethal device which contains magnesium powder and fulminate of mercury. When the ring is pulled and the grenade thrown the fulminate of mercury explodes and produces a loud bang, igniting the magnesium and producing a blinding flash of up to 50,000 candela. The two effects are sufficient to disorientate an unprotected man for up to 45 seconds.

The grenade bodies were originally made from cardboard with a minimum of metal parts to ensure that there was no danger of hostages being injured by flying metal fragments. New designs use aluminium and plastic and are configured to eject the pyrotechnic from the body of the grenade to a distance of 1 to 1.5 metres where it explodes.

Among the grenades currently available are the Condor SA GL-307, the Royal Ordnance G60 and the Haley & Weller E180 and E182.

The Haley & Weller E180 stun grenade has one charge, the E182 contains 16 sub-munitions. When the E182 is thrown the first report happens within two seconds and is followed by a succession of reports with intervals of three to four seconds.

The Haley & Weller grenades have a silent ignition system which uses a dry cell battery. When the pin has been pulled the flip-up lever is released but does not fly off and the mechanism then initiates an electric squib with a 0.5 second delay. The grenades can be command-fired or initiated by an E190 trip-wire mechanism.

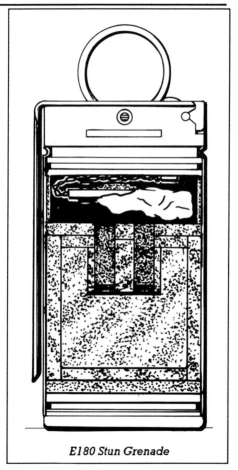

E180 Stun Grenade

Specification

Haley & Weller E180

Length: 104 mm
Diameter: 50 mm
Weight: 150 g
Nett explosive quantity: 12 g
Noise: 187 dB
Flash: 22 million candela for 10 millisecs.

Far Right Upper: The Haley & Weller Grenade Hand Stun E180

Near Right: Members of the SAS using a Haley and Weller E182 Multi Stun grenade during hostage rescue.

Far Right Lower: The Haley & Weller Grenade Hand Multi E182.

Delay Fragmentation Grenades

USA

The **M61** has been the basis for fragmentation grenades made in the UK, Brazil, Israel, South Africa and Portugal. Like the British grenade, which is designated **L2A2**, it comprises the grenade and fuze assemblies.

The grenade body consists of an explosive core (170 grams in the **L2A2**) with a threaded copper-lined fuze well. At the base of the grenade the closing cap ensures that after it has been thrown the grenade is aligned vertically so that a proper fragmentation pattern occurs. Just inside the thin metal outer casing is a notched wire coil. When the grenade explodes this coil fragments into pieces of metal about 5 mm by 1 mm, capable of injuring troops within a radius of 15 to 20 m. The small fragments inflict multiple injuries and though these may not be fatal, they shock and disable the victim. The **M61** and **L2A2** are known as 'offensive grenades' since they can be thrown by troops in the open because their casualty radius is small enough that the thrower will not be injured. 'Defensive grenades' contain larger fragments with a longer range, which make it essential that the

thrower takes cover.

The fuze is a conventional design with a split pin and fly-off handle attached to a detonator. It is screwed into the grenade body and held in place with a rubber washer. To throw the grenade, soldiers hook their index finger through the split ring and pull the split pin out of its housing; the grenade is held firmly in the other hand keeping the handle under pressure. When it is thrown the handle flips off and this releases a spring-loaded hammer which strikes a percussion cap. After a delay of 4 to 5 seconds the detonator explodes.

The grenade can be rigged as a booby-trap either by attaching a trip wire to the split ring, or by connecting a trip wire to it and placing it in a tin. The walls of the tin hold the handle down until the grenade is pulled clear by a tug on the trip wire. The grenade can also be command-detonated in an ambush.

The fuze unit may be replaced by an electric detonator, though to be completely effective it may be necessary to fill the well with a small amount of C4 or PE2 plastic explosive.

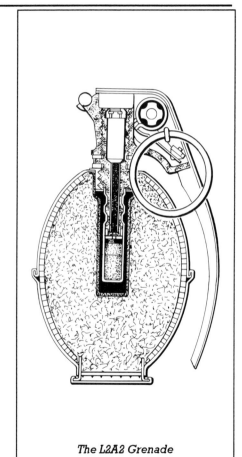

The L2A2 Grenade

Specification

M61 Delay Fragmentation Grenade

Weight: 0.45 kg
Length: 99 mm
Diameter: 57 mm
Filler: 156 grams tetryl pellets
Detonator: lead azide
Delay: 4 to 5 seconds
Manufacturer: (M61) US Army Materiel
Readiness Command, USA
(L2A2) British Aerospace Defence Ltd.,
Lancashire, UK

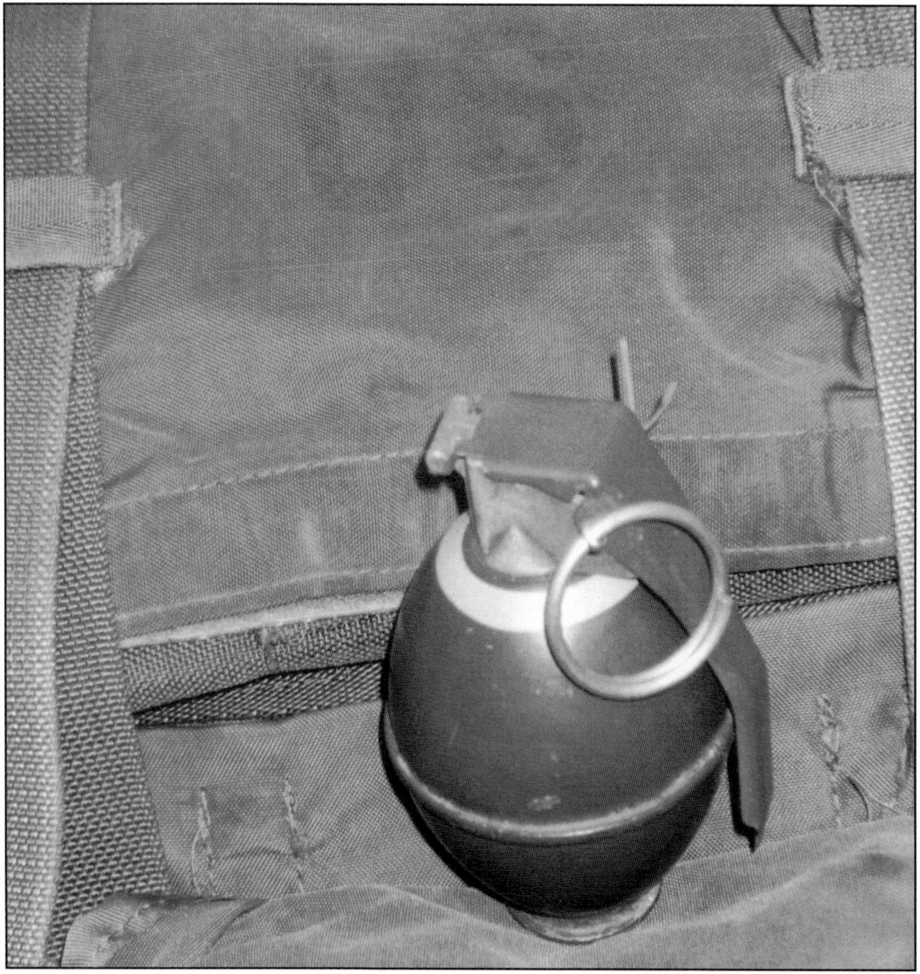

A sanitised M61, with no markings other than the yellow HE filling band, rests on a medium All-purpose Lightweight Individual Carrying Equipment (ALICE) pack.

RO BLADE Flexible Cutting Charge UK

Industrial and military targets can be attacked using simple brute force with sledge hammers or wire cutters and fire is a very effective weapon too, but explosives are the most effective since they are fast and reliable. Fitted with time delay fuzes they allow the Special Forces to be clear of the area before the explosions occur.

Plastic explosive developed during World War II is waterproof and insensitive and can be shaped around targets to ensure the maximum effect. Where the target is curved, such as a pipe or cable, an ideal charge is **Royal Ordnance Blade**.

Blade is a linear shaped charge made from DEMEX 200, an RDX based plastic explosive which detonates at 7850 metres per second. It has a copper liner to produce the metal core to the shaped charge jet. The outside of the charge is covered by a sheath of close-cell foam and, on the face that is to be attached to the target, there is a self-adhesive strip which can be cut to length with a knife.

To initiate **Blade** an L2A1/L1A1 detonator is placed in direct contact with the explosive using a pyrotechnic or electrical initiation. Lower strength detonators require a booster.

Blade can be incorporated into a conventional explosive ring-main. Whilst C2 or PE4 plastic explosive can be moulded around some targets for localised destruction, **Blade** can be deployed to cut down such targets as power and telephone poles, conduits and pipes. All the charges are linked together with detonating cord and so explode simultaneously.

There are five weights of explosive: **Blade 100** with 100 grams of DEMEX per metre, which will cut 6 mm of steel; **Blade 240** which will cut 10 mm of steel; **Blade 450** which will cut 15 mm of steel and **Blade 1150** which cut 25 mm of steel. The performance of the fifth flexible charge '**Big Blade**' is classified.

Blade 100 and **240** can cut a pipe with a 50 mm radius or make a circular hole, or trephine, with a 200 mm radius on a flat surface. **Blade 450** cuts a 300 mm trephine and **Blade 1150** a 400 mm trephine; both of the larger charges will cut a pipe with a 100 mm diameter.

Below: Generation of Blade cutting jet filmed at 1,000,000 frames per second. The shaped-charge wedge can be seen collapsing into a linear jet.

Specification

Width: 36 mm (Blade 100)
  46 mm (Blade 240)
  55 mm (Blade 450)
  79 mm (Blade 1150)
Height: 21 mm (Blade 100)
  33 mm (Blade 240)
  43 mm (Blade 450)
  58 mm (Blade 1150)
Mass of 2 m length: 0.5 kg (Blade 100)
  0.9 kg (Blade 240)
  1.5 kg (Blade 450)
  4.0 kg (Blade 1150)
Manufacturer: Royal Ordnance Industrial Energetics, Lancashire, UK

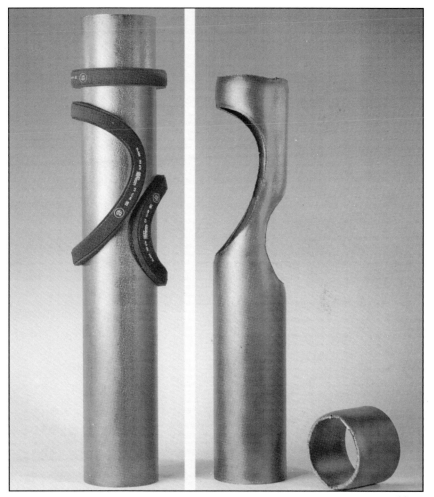

Blade linear shaped charge used against BS 1387 mild steel tube with a wall thickness of 5.4 mm and an outside diameter of 165 mm.

Simrad LP7 Handheld Laser Rangefinder   Norway

The **Simrad LP7 laser rangefinder** is about the size of a pair of 7 x 50 binoculars and weighs 2.2 kg with its battery. It gives the range accurate to five metres up to a range of 10 kilometres.

It is used by the British and Norwegian armed forces to give an accurate range for direct-fire weapons mounted on AFVs, infantry support weapons and helicopters. The most effective use of the **LP7** is for Mortar Fire Controllers (MFC) or artillery Forward Observation Officers (FOO) directing the fire of mortars or other artillery.

The range is displayed in the eyepiece and there is an indication if more than one target has been detected; unwanted reflections can be gated out by a minimum range control. Some 600 measurements can be made on the **LP7** on one charge of the 12 V rechargeable battery.

The transmitter used is a miniaturised Q-switched Nd:YAG laser. The monocular on the **LP7** has a x7 magnification and is combined with the optical receiver using a beam-splitting technique; this allows a four digit LED display to be observed through the left eyepiece, superimposed on the picture seen in the right eyepiece.

Display intensity may be adjusted by rotating the eyepiece housing. After three seconds the display is automatically shut off to preserve battery power. There is a battery and laser low-power indicator. An external power source can be used.

Options are digital setting of minimum range and built-in test and data output from the range counter. A rugged lightweight tripod with angulation head is available which provides either analogue or digital readouts of azimuth and elevation with a resolution of 5 miniradians (mrad).

The **LP7** design is reflected in the Russian Kazan 1D18 and Kazan APR-1. The US equivalent is the Litton LTL and Mark IV. The Kazan 1D18 can be used between ranges of 50 and 5000 metres, while the Litton LTL, using the eye-safe Mark V, has a range of 8 km, and 20 km with the Mark IV.

Right: Simrad LP 7 laser range finder

Specification

Simrad LP7

Dimensions: 215 x 202 x 9.3 mm
Weight: 2.2 kg (with battery)
Radiant energy: 8 mJ; 15 mJ (max)
Pulse frequency: 1 every 5 seconds,
                1 every 2 seconds
                (intermittent)
Range: 10 km
Beam width: 2 mrad
Field-of-view: 7 degrees
Magnification: x7
Manufacturer: Simrad Optronics, Norway

The Simrad LP7 in service with the Norwegian Army.

Pilkington Kite Common Weapons Sight UK

When the British Army adopted and developed the SA80 it was thought that this light and compact weapon would probably be unbalanced with the bulky and heavy Image Intensifying sight that had been fitted to the 7.62 mm Self Loading Rifle (SLR).

The technology of all image intensifying (II) sights now seems relatively simple. It takes the ambient light which is normally present from natural or man-made sources and amplifies it through a series of optical filters. These sights were first used by US forces in Vietnam - the smaller ones fitted to rifles and machine guns and the larger versions, for surveillance, mounted on tripods in armoured fighting-vehicles.

First Generation II is not now widely used since it had a tendency to 'bloom-out' or fog over if it was pointed at bright lights. Second and third generation IIs have far better image resolution and do not bloom-out.

Pilkington Optronics of North Wales addressed the problem of a new sight for the SA80 and produced one which has proved hugely successful. The **Kite,** or **Common Weapons Sight (CWS)** as it is officially designated, is made from a glass reinforced polymer, which is strong, but much lighter than earlier steel-bodied II sights. It weighs 1 kg has a x4 magnification and an 8.5 degree field-of-view. It is focused from 15 metres to infinity and using it in starlight a soldier can recognise a standing figure at 300 metres. **Kite** is in service with over 40 countries world wide.

Pilkington took the **Kite** sight and added an extra lens to the front to give it x6 magnification and a 5.5 degree field of view.

The resulting **Maxi-Kite** has the same internal features as **Kite**, but an improved performance. Both sights use two 1.5 V AA batteries as a power source. It is possible to recognise a standing figure at 450 metres. **Maxi-Kite** is ideal for snipers or larger crew-served weapons.

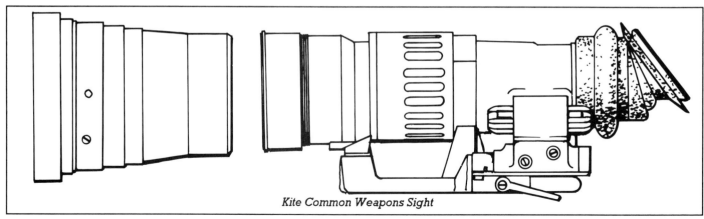

Kite Common Weapons Sight

Specification

	CWS	Maxi Kite
Weight:	1.2 kg	1.5 kg
Length:	255 mm	360 mm
Height:	80 mm	90 mm
Width:	80 mm	95 mm
Magnification	x 4	x 6

Manufacturer: Pilkington Optronics Ltd, Clwyd, Wales

The Kite Common Weapons Sight fitted to the 5.56mm SA80 rifle.

Pilkington Spyglass/HHTI Thermal Imager UK

The Pilkington Thorn Optronics **Spyglass**, also known as the Hand Held Thermal Imager or HHTI, was used by both 22 SAS in the Gulf War and also men of the 16th/5th Lancers in their reconnaissance vehicles.

The first operational use of TI was by the men of the SBS when they attacked an Argentine position at Fanning Head during the Falklands campaign in 1982. TI was used to locate the position which covered the approaches to San Carlos Bay.

Thermal Imaging presents a picture of the heat patterns by day and night generated or retained by living or inert, objects. It is therefore not dependent on ambient light from stars, moonlight or artificial sources. TI is so discriminating that it will show where a vehicle has passed, since the tracks or wheels have compressed and warmed the ground. It is particularly useful for detecting men or vehicles which may be screened by smoke, camouflage nets or vegetation because their heat will show through this cover. The original systems were bulky, almost like a small domestic TV set, with a lens at the front. However, once the technology had been proven, work was undertaken to reduce weight and size.

The **Spyglass** imager is easy to operate and can be carried slung, like a pair of binoculars. It uses modules developed from the UK Thermal Imaging Common Module (TICM) programme and is not only adaptable but has stretch capability.

Mounted on a tripod with an angulation head, **Spyglass** can be used with a laser rangefinder for fire control or target designation. Since TI is passive, the target will be unaware that it is being observed, and the brief burst of laser energy, to assess the range, may even pass unnoticed.

Spyglass is in service with all three regular British Services as well as the US Navy, US Air Force and Marine Corps. It has been adopted by the Royal Danish Air Force and Royal Netherlands Marines. It is used by the special forces of all of these nations.

Spyglass/HHTI mounted with an LP7 laser range finder.

Specification

Dimensions: 470 mm x 210 mm x 160 mm
Weight: 5 kg (with cooling air bottles and battery)
Field of view: 20 x 8.6 deg; 8 x 3.4 deg
Power consumption: 4 W (approx)
Manufacturer: Pilkington Thorn Optronics, Hayes, UK

Hand-held Thermal Imager (HHTI) known by the British Army as Spyglass in use in combat conditions.

Pilkington Optronics Lite Thermal Imager UK

Whereas Spyglass weighs 5 kg, **Lite**, which is the next generation of TI equipment, weighs about 3.5 kg and handles a little like a video camera.

The detector, which uses UK Class 1 Thermal Imaging Common Module (TICM), consists of an array of cadmium mercury telluride (CMT) photoconductive elements which can be cooled in two ways. One uses the Joule-Thompson high pressure air cooler with a re-chargeable 0.33 litre bottle, providing an operating duration of three hours at 20 degrees C. With a Lithium battery, the air cooled **Lite** weighs 4.1 kg, and is effective for five hours and 30 minutes. The second method of cooling uses a Stirling cycle microcooler which is integrated with the detector. The microcooler version weighs 3.4 kg, and with a Lithium battery has three hours' duration. Both air and microcooler versions can use an external power source.

The scanning method and imager presentation is the same as the Hand-Held Thermal Imager (HHTI) except that the user has a choice of direct viewing or display on a TV monitor. A range of interchangeable telescopic lenses can be fitted, including a selection of single and dual field-of-view options.

The low weight and bulk of **Lite** means that it can be fitted to crew-served weapons like machine-guns, and anti-tank and anti-aircraft missile firing posts. It can also be installed with the remote TI camera system to cover access points and perimeters.

Like the HHTI, the **Lite** can be fitted on a tripod with angulation head and a laser range finder similar to the Simrad LP7 and a designator similar to the Pilkington LF25. This combination allows a target to be recognised with a passive night vision system and then exposed to active laser energy for a few seconds as it is 'ranged'. As aircraft, Copperhead shells or Hellfire missiles approach, the laser designator can be activated to produce the cone shaped 'basket' of reflected laser energy into which the laser-guided-bomb or missile is targeted.

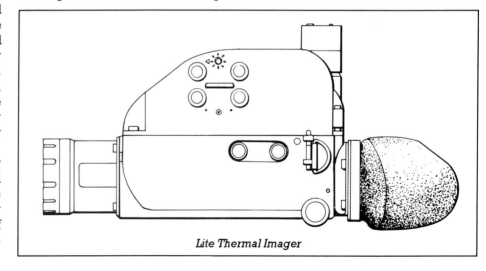

Lite Thermal Imager

Specification

Dimensions: (microcooler version)
350 x 135 x 150 mm
(aircooled version)
350 x 185 x 150 mm
Weight: (microcooler version)
3.4 kg
(aircooled version)
4.1 kg
Power consumption: 4 W (approx)
Manufacturer: Pilkington Thorn
Optronics, Hayes, UK

Seeking targets with the Pilkington Optronics Lite hand-held thermal imager.

For special forces or aircrew who may have landed far behind enemy lines it may be necessary to signal to friendly helicopters and other aircraft without using radios. Even when a radio can be used, search and rescue aircraft may have difficulty locating a single person or small group in jungle or desert.

The oldest and simplest device is the signal mirror that is made out of a stainless steel or laminated glass and has an aiming hole in the centre. The user can see the reflected sunlight through this hole when he holds the mirror to his eye and aims this light at the helicopter or other aircraft as it approaches.

The instructions on the US Air Force mirror advise that it should be used even when an enemy aircraft or ship is not in sight, since the flash of light can be seen for many miles. Mirrors can be improvised from the inside of the metal lid of survival kit.

Signal mirrors were particularly effective in Vietnam where smoke grenades, that had been thrown to call in helicopters, also attracted North Vietnamese or Viet Cong troops.

Smoke and miniflares can be used to attract attention, but they are of short duration. **The Schermuly Day and Night Signal No. 1 Mk. 4** however is a versatile waterproof pyrotechnic that weighs 228 g, is 139 mm long and has an orange smoke marker at one end and a flare at the other. The flares are covered by red protective screw caps and operated by a pull ring. Raised ribs on the body of the signal indicate the smoke end, so the device can be used in complete darkness.

The smoke burns for 18 seconds and is used by day. The red flare lasts for 12 seconds and has a light intensity of over 10,000 candela.

The strobe light that is carried by air crew is also a standard item of equipment with special forces like the US Navy SEALS. They have the compact waterproof **ACR Firefly Rescue Lite**, which weighs 212.5 g. The lite is sewn into a pouch on their battle dress uniform.

A strobe light will pulse for up to 24 hours with a strength of 200,000 candela which can be visible up to five kilometres away.

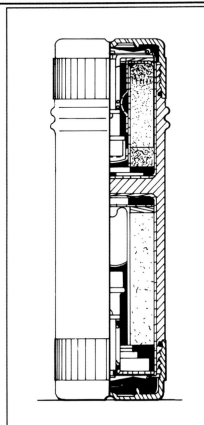

The Schermuly Day & Night Signal No. 1 Mk. 4

Specification

Day and Night Signal No. 1 Mk 4

Length: 139 mm
Width: 42.5 mm
Weight: 228 g
Explosive content: 93 g
Smoke burn time: 18 seconds
Flare burn time: 20 seconds at 10,000 candela
Manufacturer: Schermuly, High Post, Salisbury UK

A British soldier demonstrates the signal mirror - the oldest emergency signalling device.

The ACR Firefly Rescue Lite as used by the US Navy SEALS.

LF25 Man-portable Laser Designator   UK

Laser designators, such as the Hughes AN/PAQ-1 and AN/PAQ-3 Mule, in service with the US Marine Corps and Army, give men on the ground a system which allows them to deliver airborne ordnance, the Paveway and Pavetack Laser-Guided Bombs (LGBs), onto ground targets with very high accuracy. These 746 kg or 1119 kg 'smart' bombs, as opposed to unguided 'iron' or 'dumb' bombs, were first used in Vietnam against the Than Hoa road and rail bridge south of Hanoi. The bridge had been attacked several times but never destroyed. On April 27th, 1972 it was badly damaged by F-4 Phantom fighter-bombers, armed with smart bombs, and finally destroyed on May 13th, 1972 in operation Linebacker 1. Designation of the target was undertaken by an aircraft.

LGBs were used at the close of the campaign in the Falklands Islands in 1982 when, from a position on Wireless Ridge, a Forward Air Controller (FAC) designated an Argentine artillery position for Harriers. He chose as his target, for the laser designator, the helmet of one of the Argentine soldiers since the metal would give a strong reflection.

LGBs were used extensively in the Gulf War in 1991. The US Army employed Copperhead 155 mm laser-guided shells to destroy Iraqi observation towers on the border. In Bosnia, British Special Forces used designators to allow Sea Harriers to attack point targets. Later, when the NATO air campaign was launched against Serb positions, point targets were attacked with LGBs.

The **Pilkington LF25 designator** weighs only 8 kg and can therefore be carried by a soldier in its transit case, or in his rucksack. It has an integral x 10 telescope through which the laser output and receive and sighting channels are multiplexed. Power is provided by either a lithium or rechargeable Nicad battery.

The **LF 25** can designate targets up to 10 kilometres away. It uses solid state slab-laser geometry which requires no liquid cooling nor warm-up prior to operation.

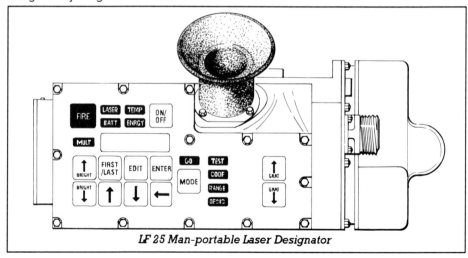

LF 25 Man-portable Laser Designator

Specification

Pilkington LF25

Weight: 6 kg
Output energy: >80mJ
Beam divergence: <0.25 mrad
Range: min 300 m; max 9995 m
Field of view: 3 degrees
Magnification: x 10
Manufacturer: Barr & Stroud Ltd,
Glasgow, UK

The Pilkington LF25 man-portable laser designator.

Paratrooper's Gravity Blade Knife   Germany

Prior to World War II, when the German parachute force was a separate arm under the control of the Luftwaffe, it received a lavish amount of equipment. One of the items was a **gravity blade knife** which was carried in a special button-flapped pocket in the combat trousers.

The principle of such knives is that the blade telescopes into the handle and is held in place by a spring-loaded catch. To operate it the catch is pressed and the blade drops out under the force of gravity, and the catch then locks it open.

The knives were issued to paratroopers in case they became entangled with their parachutes upon landing and had only one hand free. They could then operate the knife and cut themselves out of their harness. The knife also had an 80 mm spike which could be used for untangling rigging lines when, following an operational jump, parachutes were being re-packed on the ground. Where the guard would be on a conventional knife these have a hook

designed to accommodate rigging lines.

When the new West German Army, the Bundeswehr, was established in 1956 it again adopted the **gravity blade knife** for airborne and armoured troops.

Ordinary soldiers had a functional pocket knife with a saw blade and other utility features. The handle of the post-war **gravity blade knife** was made from chequered grey-green plastic, unlike the elegant hardwood of the earlier knives. In other respects the knife was identical to its war-time counterpart.

Manufacturers included W.M.F. and later Eickhorn, both cutlers based in Solingen.

The knife is popular with all NATO special forces who trade or buy it as a versatile working blade. It is normally carried in a webbing pouch on the soldier's belt order.

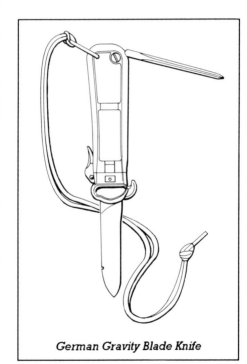

German Gravity Blade Knife

Specification

Length closed: 135 mm
Length open: 220 mm
Spike: 80 mm
Blade: 85 mm
Weight: 245 grams
Manufacturer: Eickhorn, Solingen, Germany

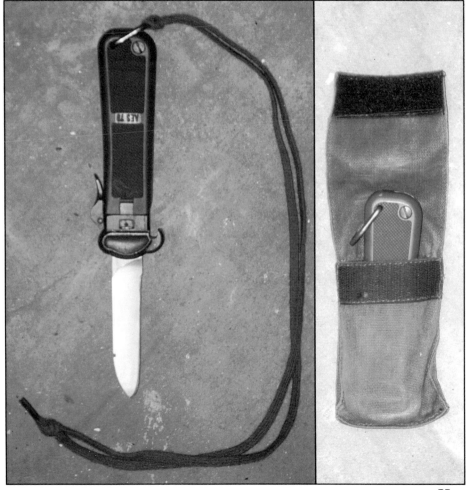

Near Right: The Eickhorn manufactured gravity blade knife with blade deployed. It is a compact and robust pocket knife widely favoured by special forces.

Far Right: German paratrooper's gravity blade knife in pouch.

In World War II British special forces used the Fairbairn-Sykes (FS) commando dagger. It was a double edged weapon based on a shape first used in Ancient Egypt. The FS is perpetuated in the blue and red British Army All Arms Commando badge. At about the same time the US Marine Corps adopted a single edged combat knife that was first manufactured by the Ka-Bar Cutlery Company and became widely known as the K-bar. Its correct designation was Knife, Hunting 7 inch w/Sheath. It has a black full tang parkerised blade with a handle made of compressed leather washers. By 1965 knives were manufactured by the Camillus Company (USMC Knife) of the USA with a black sheath and handle. The US Air Force Aircrew Survival knife that entered service in the 1960s has remained a firm favourite with special forces. It has a 1025 mm saw backed blade and a sharpening stone in a separate pouch.

In the 1980s the Ontario Company of the USA produced the Spec Plus range of US combat knives. They replaced the leather sheaths with Cordura and configured the press stud fittings so that the knife could be worn upside down on the harness of load-carrying equipment. The full tang blades were retained but embedded in rubber composite handles, which would not rot in jungle conditions and were easier to handle in extreme cold. The Spec Plus range included the stainless steel US Navy combat knife, Air Crew Survival knife and the Marine or "Ka-Bar".

In the United Kingdom British forces are equipped with a robust 31 cm survival knife. It has a wooden grip, full tang parkerised 18 cm blade, and weighs 680 grams and a riveted leather sheath.

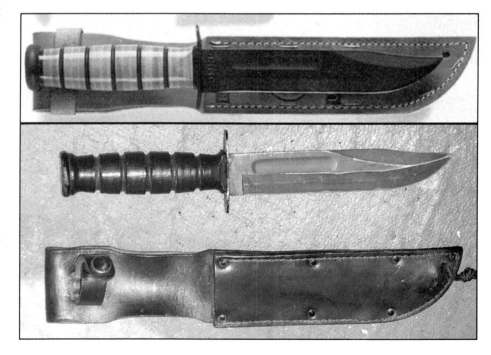

Specification

Knife Hunting 7 inch (Ka-Bar)
Weight: 4.5 grams
Blade length: 178 mm
Overall length: 3050 mm
Rockwell hardness: C 56-58
Manufacturers: Ka-Bar Cutlery Company;
Ontario Company (Spec Plus); Camillus
Company (USMC), USA

Left Upper: *The Ka-Bar fighting knife as used by the US Marine Corps and SEALS.*

Left Lower: *The Camillus seven inch Marine knife.*

Right: *An Ontario Spec Plus Marine knife in a customised sheath attached to a belt order.*

Crimpers and Multi-tools USA

The United States has pioneered a range of folding pocket sized multi-tools that have been adopted by Special Forces world wide. During World War II the Allied special forces like the OSS and SOE were issued with a combination pocket knife and spanner/wrench, but it was not until the late 1970s that the concept again found favour with special forces. The attraction of these tools is that they enable a soldier to undertake precise work which would be beyond the scope of a combat knife that, at best, will have a wire cutter and saw in the heavy blade and screwdriver in the scabbard.

The oldest multi-tool, in what is now a wide range, is the **Leatherman Survival Tool**, which has a full-sized set of pliers/wire cutters, four screwdrivers (small, medium, large and Phillips), a file, awl/punch, can and bottle opener, 635 mm knife blade, and an eight inch ruler.

The most popular version for special forces is in black and has a cut-out in the pliers so that it can be used to crimp non-electric detonators or blasting caps.

SOG in the United States have produced the Power Plier and Paratool. The latter is available in black and users

can change the blades by unscrewing hex nuts in the handle.

Gerber, who are famous for a range of combat knives, also produce a folding tool in stainless steel and black, called the Multiplier. Like the SOG tool it can be modified with different tools. The user can open the Multiplier with one hand.

Leatherman have also produced the PST II or **Pocket Survival Tool II** that weighs only 142 grams. Among its tools are scissors and a file with a diamond coating. The Leatherman Super Tool is 113 grams heavier than the standard Pocket Survival Tool, but in addition to the same tools it has an electrical crimper, serrated blade, wire stripper and a wood/bone saw.

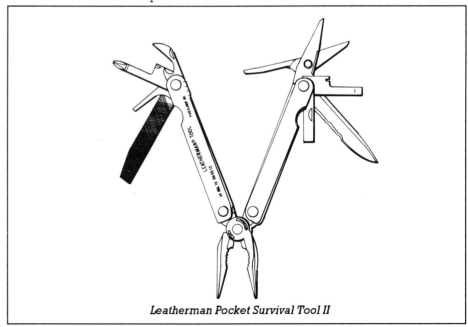

Leatherman Pocket Survival Tool II

Specification

Leatherman Pocket Survival Tool II

Length closed: 1000 mm
Length open: 1500 mm (with full-size pliers)
Width, closed: 2.25 mm
Width, open: 150 mm
Depth: 14 mm
Weight: 142 g
Rockwell hardness: C 57-59
Manufacturer: Leatherman Tool Group Inc, Portland, Oregon, USA

A soldier cuts D10 signals cable with a Leatherman Pocket Crimper Survival Tool.

Silva Model 27 Compass

All members of special forces carry a survival kit that is small enough to fit into a pocket in their combat clothing. If they are forced to relinquish their rucksack and belt order - the former carrying the essentials for living in the field and the latter those for fighting - they can still survive using the compact kit they carry with them.

The contents vary according to the individual soldier, but some essentials are: a compass, waterproof matches, a candle (a tallow that can be used for cooking), a flint for producing sparks, fishhook and line, snare wire, wire saw, scalpel blades, and a condom which is capable of carrying up to a litre of water. Also included is a first aid kit which contains water sterilising tablets, antibiotics, potassium permanganate, analgesic and antihistamine tablets as well as plasters and butterfly sutures. Butterfly sutures will hold a wound together in a similar way to stitches.

A compass is an essential part of the kit and the **Silva Model 40 SERE** - (Survival, Evasion, Resistance Escape) is a tiny button compass with a circumference of 18 mm and diameter of 5.6 mm. It shows the eight cardinal points and is available in both luminous and non-luminous versions.

However, the most useful survival compass is the **Silva Model 27** that has been adopted by NATO. The compass has a lid with a mirror which when half open reflects the compass card and so can be used for taking bearings. This facility can also be used for establishing the time. The user takes the bearing on the sun and then turns the compass over and through the transparent base reads where the North direction arrow points on the clock face.

The **Model 27** has a safety-pin that allows it to be fixed to a combat jacket so the user has both hands free, but can make quick checks on his bearing.

The **Model 27** can be opened fully and used with a map as a protractor to give bearings for the legs of a cross country move.

Silva Model 27 Compass

Specification

Graduation: Available in 360° or 6400'
Illumination: Zinc-sulphide compound
Baseplate markings: mm
Size: 108 x 42 x 11 mm (folded 58 x 42 x 14 mm)
Accuracy: +/- 1.0 degrees (+/- 17.5 mils)
Weight: 22 g
Manufacturer: Silva AB, Sollentuna, Sweden

The Model 27 Survival may also be used as a protractor as a navigational aid.

The tiny size of the Model 27 can be seen in this soldier's hand.

All soldiers have a first field-dressing, either carried in a pouch on the All-purpose Lightweight Individual Carrying Equipment (ALICE) load carrying harness, or taped to the weapon. It is common to carry two dressings since a rifle bullet causes an exit as well as an entry wound.

The US armed forces are also issued with a nylon First Aid Kit, individual pouch which soldiers attach to the middle of the back of their ALICE belts. This was originally a US Marine Corps item, but is now used throughout the forces. Inside the pouch a plastic box, **'Insert, First Aid Kit Case'** holds a range of basic first aid equipment. This includes iodine, eye dressings with ointment, plasters, a triangular bandage for supporting injured arms, first field dressing, water purifying tablets, lip salve and cleaning swabs. In the field the olive drab triangular bandage is often used as a bandanna/sweat rag.

There is also a card with instructions on mouth-to-mouth resuscitation. Plastic vials are included for analgesic tablets.

For a soldier the attraction of the kit is that he can mix and match its contents according to the perceived threats in the area of operations; blood volume expanding fluid, for rehydrating wounded or heat-exhausted soldiers; morphine,

penicillin tablets, scalpel and blades, suture strips, and diarrhoea tablets are among the extras that can be carried.

US Special Forces Medical NCOs carry an M3 kit and a minor surgery kit. The surgical kit contains a suture set, prep pads, suture scissors, bandage scissors, scalpel blade and handle, two Kelly forceps, tweezers and a pen light in a toolkit style pouch. A Medical NCO using

an air-droppable laboratory, X-ray and dental equipment could set up and operate a small hospital and dispensary in the most remote parts of the world.

The SAS and the US Special Forces have discovered that medical assistance to remote tribes is a very effective way of 'winning the hearts and minds' and so ensuring a steady supply of local intelligence.

Specification

First Aid Kit Individual

Height: 110 mm
Width: 50 mm
Depth: 50 mm
Weight: 500 to 600 g according to contents
Attachment points: ALICE clips to belt, or Velcro loops to harness
Manufacturer: Contents from several pharmaceutical companies

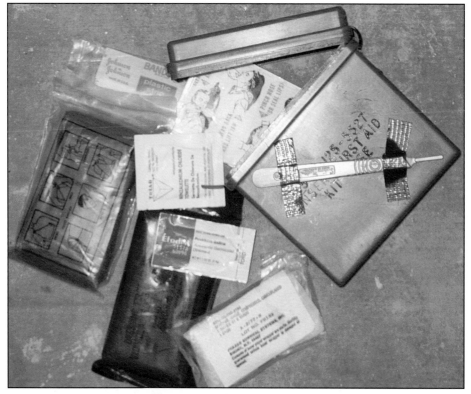

The compact First Aid Kit Individual pouch showing contents.

Opposite: *US Army Individual First Aid Kit pouch and inner container.*

Body Armour

The development of Kevlar in the United States led to dramatic changes in body armour design. Armour protection against small arms ammunition and shell and grenade fragments had been worn since World War I, but used steel plates, which were heavy and inflexible. Kevlar is an aramid fibre which can be woven as a flexible mesh of fibres or be incorporated into shields and helmets; it can absorb and dissipate the energy of a bullet, or fragment.

Body armour was widely used in the Vietnam War and has now become the almost universal equipment for front-line soldiers. It is also worn by VIPs who may be potential targets for assassination attempts. The protection is incorporated into a waistcoat or worn discreetly under a shirt. Special Forces in hostage rescue operations wear it with helmets and respirators.

Military or Police body armour normally includes a collar, adjustable velcro closures and a range of pockets to take magazines and radio equipment. The SAS wear armour from Bristol Engineering and Armourshield. The latter's GPV 25 is worn for hostage rescue operations and will defeat .357 Magnum, 9 mm and 7.62 mm bullets.

In the United States, RBR Armor produces six types of body armour. The 100 series provides ballistic protection under shirts, and the 101 vest also has anti-stab protection. The 200 series are Police overvests and include a SWAT vest suitable for hostage rescue operations. The 300 series are military vests including the 302 which is the US armed forces PASGT and the 304 which is the British Army Combat Body Armour. The 400 series includes the 405, a combat swimmer vest which has water resistant armour and waterproof panels. The 500 series are covert overvests and include the 501, a quilted 'body warmer'. The 800 series provide heavy protection for Explosive Ordnance Device (EOD) disposal.

Hard armour like RBR 'Armour Light', German Standard SK2 steel plates and ceramic plates are heavier than flexible armours but will defeat hits by high velocity ammunition.

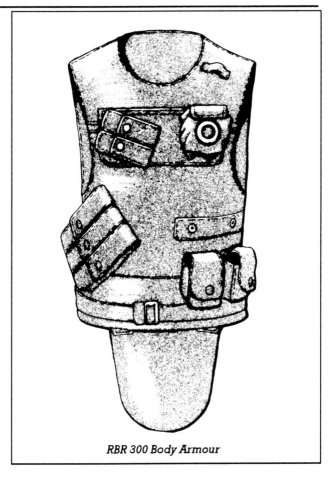

RBR 300 Body Armour

Specification

RBR Armour Light

Height: 300 mm
Width: 250 mm
Weight: 1.8 kg
Performance: It will defeat 6 strikes at a minimum distance between strikes of 50 mm by 5.56 mm M193 at 1000 m/s; 5.56 mm SS109 at 1000 m/s and 7.62 mm x 51 .308 Win Ball at 853 m/s
Manufacturer: RBR Armour Inc , Pennsylvania, USA

200 series Special Weapons and Tactics (SWAT) vest.

S10 Anti-gas Respirator

In a hostage rescue operation the Special Forces aim to overwhelm the terrorists before they can kill or injure the hostages. However, the dilemma is that the indiscriminate use of lethal force can cause death and injury to those people that the Special Forces are attempting to rescue. CS gas and Stun Grenades, as well as very accurate small arms fire, have proved effective in a number of operations. However to enjoy the advantage that the gas and blinding explosions give the rescuers, they must be protected against their effect.

At the Iranian Embassy the SAS wore the S6 respirator, which has since been superseded by the **S10.** The S6 had curved eye pieces which gave the wearer good visibility, but were not compatible with night vision equipment like the CWS and Lite. The **S10** has round eyepieces which work well with optical equipment; and it also has a built in drinking tube which allows the wearer to drink water from a special seal in his water bottle top without removing the mask.

The filter canister on the **S10** can be replaced with a collective filtration unit. The haversack for the respirator has pockets for decontamination equipment, nerve agent tablets and auto-inject pens.

The **SF10** is a respirator designed for Special Forces. It has provision for an internal microphone which is used with a communications harness/radio transmitter and ear defenders. The microphone replaces the drinking tube facility. The mask can be fitted with a second filter canister, which allows it to be used by left or right handed shooters; this can be used to give the wearer oxygen without the mask being removed. The eyepieces can be fitted with tinted lenses which protect against the flash of stun grenades and any small fragments, but which can be quickly removed by hand after the initial assault.

The **AR10** is a police model which is in service with the majority of police firearm units in the UK.

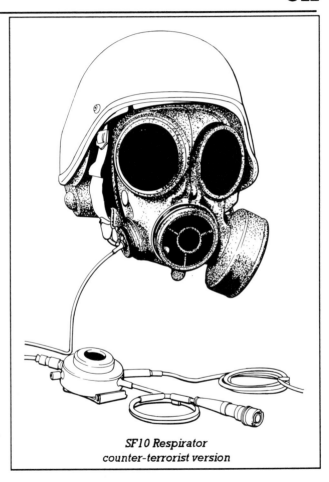

*SF10 Respirator
counter-terrorist version*

Specification

S110 Anti Gas Respirator

Weight: <800 g (with filter)
Protection: All warfare gases and aerosols, radioactive dust
Canister thread: STANAG 4155
Total leakage: <0.0%
Donning time: <9 secs.
Breathing resistance: With L12A1 NBC filter canister inhalation 460 Pa at 89 litres/min, exhilation 85 Pa at 80 litres/min
Eyepieces: High scratch resistant coated polycarbonate
Drinking rate: >100 millilitres/min
Life cycle: 20 years
Manufacturer: Protection Group, Avon Industries Ltd. Melksham, UK

The S10 respirator worn with charcoal cloth nuclear biological and chemical warfare clothing (NBC).

In a hostage rescue operation even the shortest delay can mean the death of one or more of the hostages. If they are held in a locked building, the doors or windows and even the walls are a point of access. Explosives fitted to a portable frame can be used to blast a way in, but may cause casualties to those inside. The SAS used frame charges to gain access to the Iranian Embassy at Princes Gate on 5th May 1980, but knew where the hostages were held.

If there is a requirement for silence or if explosives present a risk, manual, hydraulic and pneumatic door rams can be used exerting a force from 3.04 tonnes through 5.08 to 11.17 tonnes.

An alternative is the door ripper which uses a blade driven between the door and frame, close to the lock mechanism, with the aid of a club hammer or manual door ram. Pulling back hard on the handle will force the door open, normally at the first attempt. If there is resistance this can be overcome by using the ratchet mechanism in the handle which allows the blade to be worked behind the door to improve the effectiveness of the applied force.

The manual door ram weighs 16 kg and is swung by one man against the door in the lock area. It opens all but steel-reinforced doors.

The hydraulic door ram is designed to open reinforced inward opening doors. When in position, with the main ram over the lock area, a secondary ram is first activated to force the jaws deep into the frame. By opening a valve the main ram is activated to force the door open with a force of up to 5.08 tonnes.

The pneumatic door ram is first positioned on the door with the air-bag support-plate over the lock area. The hydraulic claws are then forced into the door frame with the hand pump to provide secure anchoring. The air-bag is placed between the plate and the door and inflated using the portable compressed-air cylinder. Doors open in less than a second.

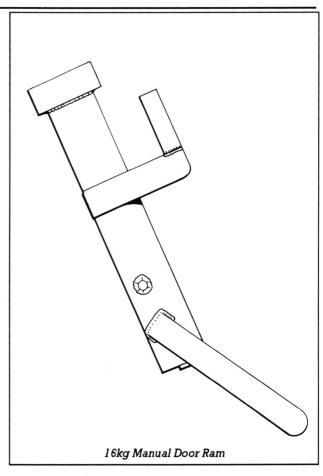

16kg Manual Door Ram

Specification

Manual door ram
Force: 3.04 tonnes

Hydraulic door ram
Force: 5.08 tonnes

Pneumatic door ram
Force: 11.17 tonnes

Manufacturer: P.W. Allen, Evesham, UK

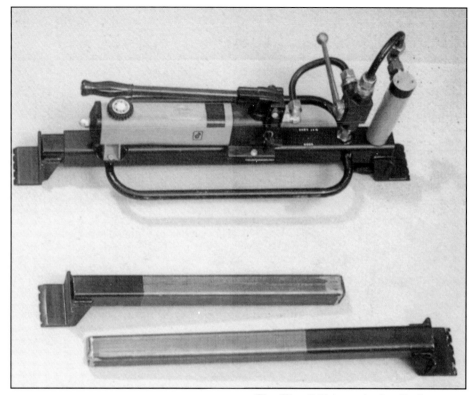

The Allen 5.08 tonne hydraulic door ram.

Global Positioning System (GPS)

Global Positioning System is based on 24 US NAVSTAR satellites which have a span of 5.2 metres with solar panels extended. They weigh 860 kg and circle the world at a height of 20,000 kilometres making one circumnavigation every twelve hours. They provide an all weather, common grid world-wide navigation and timing information service to land, sea and air and even to space travellers. Users enter the way stations or grid or longitude and latitude check points on their proposed course into the **GPS**. An arrow displayed on the screen of a Swedish Silva hand-held **GPS** shows whether the user should move to left or right to remain on course, as well as giving the course correction in degrees. It also shows the bearing to the way point and its distance from the user. This level of accuracy is ensured by fixes on four or more of the NAVSTAR satellites.

The lead on the programme came from the US Air Force. It was a crucial aid for Special Forces during the Gulf War in 1991 when navigation, particularly at night, was very difficult in the desert. It had, however, entered service almost ten years earlier when the Royal Navy deployed to the South Atlantic to liberate the Falklands.

Following the Gulf War, the US Army, which, prior to 1991, had thought it would only be useful for helicopter navigation, stated that it had a requirement for 350 one channel manpacked/vehicle sets; 63 five-channel sea sets and 4949 two-channel aircraft sets. In addition their request for an additional 50,764 commercial-grade sets and 880 aircraft sets was approved by the Department of the Army in April.

Two American companies, Trimble and Magellan, have dominated the military and commercial **GPS** field. Trimble equipment includes the Centurion which is installed in AFVs and helicopters and the Miniature Underwater GPS Receiver (MUGR), which is waterproof to 20 metres, has six channels and is the smallest hand held receiver weighing only 0.54 kg.

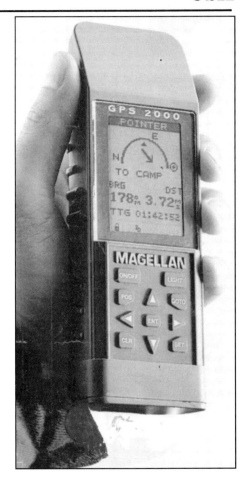

Magellan GPS 2000 system

Specification

Magellan GPS 2000

Waypoint storage: 100
Navigation leg storage: 29
Weight: 280 g
Dimensions: 5.8 cm x 3.3 cm x 16.8 cm
Power supply: 4 AA Akaline batteries
Battery life: 17 hours continuous use
Accuracy: 15 metres
Manufacturer: Magellan Systems
Corporation, San Dimas, USA

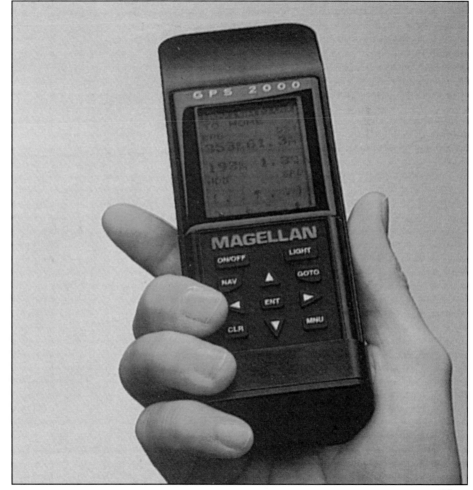

The compact Magellan GPS 2000, a pocket-sized navigation aid.

The United States pioneered work on ground sensors during the Vietnam War when they air dropped, or hand emplaced, them along the Ho Chi Minh trail in Cambodia and Laos. The operation, code-named Igloo White, allowed US Air Force aircraft flying over the area to pick up the signals transmitted by these devices. The Unattended Ground Sensors (UGS) and Air Delivered Seismic Intrusion Devices (ADSIDs) showed if wheeled-traffic or foot-soldiers were moving down the trail. There is a report that the USAF recorded transmissions from an acoustic device which was a conversation between two North Vietnamese soldiers discussing what they should do with the device!

Since the Vietnam War the United States has refined its remote sensor systems and produced the Martin Marietta REMBASS (REmotely Monitored BAttlefield Sensor System) and the Improved version IREMBASS.

In the United Kingdom Racal produced CLASSIC (Covert Local Area Sensor System for Intrusion Classification). Like REMBASS it has been improved and enhanced since it was introduced. For Special Forces CLASSIC is a force multiplier since it allows a small force to monitor movement over a wide area and pass this intelligence back to headquarters.

CLASSIC consists of the TA2781 Sensor Unit which has a miniaturised radio with a range of up to 21 km and a battery life of 90 days. It is linked to either the MA2743 seismic, MA2744 passive IR, MA2770 magnetic or MA2772 piezoelectric cable sensors. When they detect movement the TA2781 transmits to the RA2786 monitor unit which gives an audio or visual display. A ruggedised printer is available to give a real-time record of movements. If the information is being displayed in a secure HQ, an MA2775 data interface can show it on a computer-generated map.

The seismic system has a range of between one and 150 metres, depending on ground conditions, and will identify personnel and wheeled or tracked vehicles.

The passive IR beam on the MA2744 has two direction paths and can therefore indicate which direction a man or vehicle is moving. It has a range of 60 metres but

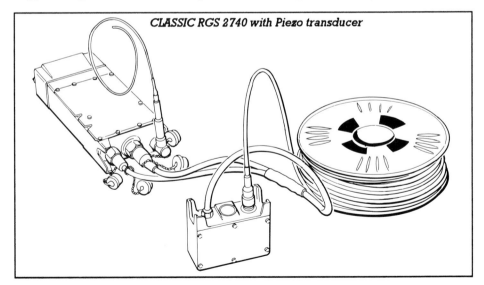

CLASSIC RGS 2740 with Piezo transducer

will pick up vehicles out to 300 metres

The MA2770 magnetic unit will pick up the mass of a vehicle and, if two units are emplaced, will give direction. At five to 20 metres it will detect cars, at 10 to 40 metres, tracked vehicles; whilst between one and ten metres it can indicate whether a weapon is being carried.

The MA 2772 piezoelectric cable is dug into the ground just below the surface and will stretch for up to 750 metres. The high sensitivity cable will detect personnel, while the low sensitivity cable will indicate vehicle movement; with two cables the direction of vehicles and personnel can be detected.

The CLASSIC TA2781 can also be used with pressure pads, contact closure switches, trip wires, inertia switches and NBC sensors. With the RTA2785 Relay Unit the range of the TA2781 can be increased up to 30 km.

Specifications:

Sensor:
Size: 95 mm x 250 mm x 42 mm
Weight: 1.3 kg

Monitor:
Size: 95 mm x 250 mm x 42 mm
Weight: 1.3 kg

Relay:
Size: 95 mm x 250 mm x 42 mm
Weight: 1.4 kg

Manufacturer: Racal Comsec, Salisbury, UK.

An infantry patrol passes an MA2743 seismic detection device with its TA2781 sensor unit.

93

Experience of co-ordinating emergency and security agencies has shown that most of them do not use radio communications equipment which is compatible. Thus special forces, who may be confronting the same threat, may be unable to liaise on the radio net because they use radios working on different wavebands or frequencies. These problems can be compounded if fire and ambulance crews are brought into a major incident. In the past the solution was to duplicate radios - with Army, Police and Emergency Service operators working side by side. It was wasteful of man-power, slow and potentially insecure. The solution was the

Racal Cougarnet.

Cougarnet uses a series of talk-through outstations providing communications within a designated area. If the operational need requires a bigger net, these talk-throughs can be combined to produce a single channel of all information. Talk-through stations can be static - or mobile so that they can be moved to an incident.

Cougarnet is based around two main equipments: a synthesiser-controlled hand-held radio and an amplifier appliqué unit to provide increased power. Both units are available in VHF and UHF and a wide range of ancillary equipment enables the build-up of a powerful,

versatile and flexible network.

The latest equipment in this range is the **Cougar 2000 mobile radio VRM 5110 HS/US** which can be fitted to military vehicles or Police cars. Blank front panel variants (VRM 5110 HB or UB) can be fitted into unmarked cars for covert operations. The radio is then controlled from the fully sealed Covert Control Unit (MA 5112). Separate units cover VHF 136-174 MHz and UHF 440-512 MHz frequency bands. The RF output is programmable between pre-set high and low power settings of 10-25W and 0.5-2W. The radios support 99 channels and have channel scanning and cloning as standard with encryption as an option.

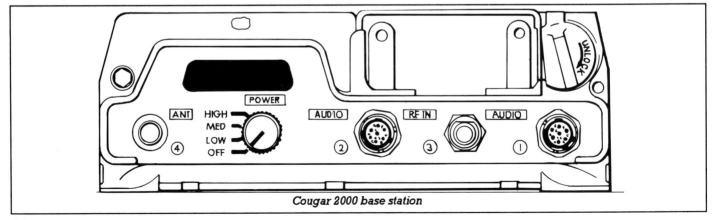

Cougar 2000 base station

Specification

Cougar 2000

Fequency range: VHF 136 - 174 MHz,
UHF 440 - 512 MHz
Height: 50 mm
Width: 179 mm
Depth: 230 mm
Weight: 25 kg

Sending on the Cougarnet communications system using the mobile talk-through outstation.

Receiving on the Cougarnet communications system using the hand-held transceiver.

The first frequency-hopping radios produced by Racal were the Jaguar V and hand-held Caracal series. Continuing the big cat tradition their latest is the **Panther**.

The smallest is the **Panther 2000-P**, a hand-held radio which weighs only 1.1 kg. The attraction of a radio like the **2000-P** and earlier Caracal is that they give secure communications, albeit over relatively short ranges. The short range is not a problem, since either a relay or more powerful radio is likely to be within range.

The **2000-P** is ideal for a close-range reconnaissance work where bulk and weight would impose a serious penalty on movement, or where a senior officer has left his vehicle, but wishes to communicate by a secure means.

The **2000-P** has a frequency range from between 30 and 87.97 MHz. It uses 1 Watt of power which ensures reliable communications, long battery life and a low probability of intercept. In the frequency-hopping mode it can switch between 2320 channels.

The **Panther 2000-V** is the smallest and lightest Electronic Counter-Measures (ECM) manpack radio available. It provides 3120 channels at 25 kHz spacing and can operate in three modes to send speech or data, fixed frequency clear, fixed frequency secure using the built in 16 kbit/s digital encryption and frequency-hopping secure speech and data. If a radio is operating in the frequency-hopping mode it can be contacted through a 'hailing' system by a fixed frequency radio which alerts the operator to tune into the fixed frequency.

Among the options available for **Panther** is Over The Air Rekeying (OTAR), which allows the frequency-hopping codes to be inserted. If a radio is captured, individual radios can be barred from the net through a selective calling facility, which allows one-to-one communication.

The **Panther 200-H** is a HF set which provides power outputs of 5, 25 or 50 watts in the manpack role and up to 100 or 400 watts in a vehicle or base station. It operates between 1.5 and 30 MHz in 100 Hz steps and hops between frequencies ten times a second, it can be used for standard fixed frequency voice and Carrier Wave (CW-Morse). When in its frequency agile mode it can be used on a net or station to station.

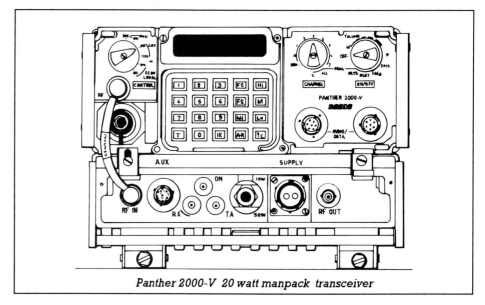

Panther 2000-V 20 watt manpack transceiver

Specification:

Panther 2000-V

Frequency range: 30 - 108 MHz
Height: 90 mm
Width: 230 mm
Depth: 205 mm
Weight: 4.5 kg

The Panther 2000-V man pack frequency agile radio.

UK/VSC-501 Satellite Communications UK

The **VSC-501** is a vehicle-borne tactical SATCOM system working in the military SHF band of 7.25 to 8.4 GHz via a geostationary satellite. It may be assembled in about 15 minutes by a two-man crew, but in an emergency this can be done by one man. The **VSC-501** is carried in a Fitted For Radio (FFR) Land Rover 110 and powered from the 24 volt DC source in the vehicle. Between locations the equipment can remain switched on to enable it to be brought into action very quickly. The **VSC-501** can be used for speech, telegraph and data.

The dish, which is 1.9 metres in diameter, is composed of four petals which couple together prior to fixing to a quadrupod mount. It can be operated in winds up to 20 metres per second on ground sloping at 15 degrees, without ballast.

Once it has been assembled the station can be supervised by one man. His duties consist of switching speech circuits over the satellite link, manning the on-board telegraph circuit, monitoring the equipment functions and providing other channels to remote users.

A typical station configuration might comprise the following: a 16 kbit channel, switched and encrypted on-board providing a secure speech facility; a 2.4 kbit channel, providing a high speed data circuit to a remote user; and an insecure telegraph EOW channel terminated on board. There could also be three other remote-user telegraph channels of which one is encrypted on-board and the other two encrypted at remote user terminals.

During the final surrender negotiations in Stanley, Falkland Islands, in 1982, the Argentine officers asked the Spanish speaking Royal Marine officer to whom the British radio operator, with a manpack radio set, was speaking, "He is speaking to London" said the Royal Marine to the startled Argentine officers. The messages and replies were being passed back to a SATCOM station on one of the mountains on the island and thence back to Downing Street, in London!

Specification

Frequency range: 7.25-7.75 GHz (downlink)
7.9 - 8.4 GHz (uplink)
Diameter: 1.9 m
Power supply: 24 volts DC
Maximum power requirement: 1.5 kW at 28V DC
Manufacturer: Racal Communications, Reading, UK

Opposite: Two photographs showing a parts layout and assembly of Racal VSC-501 satcom system.

A satellite dish set up and in one-man deployment, under camouflage.

Electronic Warfare

Special Forces are usually used for direct action, hostage rescue, assaults on enemy key points and the like, but,they may also be used simply to gather intelligence. This work may be undertaken in counter-insurgency or counter-terrorist campaigns or within the context of a conventional war. In counter-insurgency or counter-terrorist operations Special Forces may work in civilian clothes in unmarked cars within a city. The attic of a derelict house or a flat in a tower-block may become an OP equipped with video and stills cameras and tape recorders, together with log books and photo-files on suspects and their vehicles. Working in a city carries a great risk of detection and discovery, but it does have the advantage that teams are protected from the weather in buildings or vehicles.

They may also undertake surveillance work in the country and here they will be carefully camouflaged in hides or OPs similar to those used by naturalists for wild-life programmes. This can be testing for patience and stamina as they must wait, almost without moving, in all weathers. Their food must be eaten cold so that smells cannot be detected and all traces of the occupation of the hide, including human waste, are bagged-up and removed at the close of the operation.

In conventional war the information requirement changes. Instead of reporting back to Police and Army HQs on terrorist sitings and movements, the close-reconnaissance team will be logging weapons and equipment. They will note where they are sited and report on the routines of the guard or garrison. This information may be passed back directly to a Corps HQ where it will be used to build up an intelligence picture for subsequent operations. During the Falklands War, 22 SAS were able to send information back to the UK, via a satellite link,

when finally the Argentine commander, General Menendez, agreed to discuss surrender. The British Government was kept abreast of these developments via this link throughout the campaign.

In the days of the Cold War it was assumed that Special Forces would man pre-sited hides in Soviet territory as Soviet and Warsaw Pact troops drove westwards towards Germany and that from these hides they would watch the movement of enemy vehicles. This information was to be used for tasking the crews of A-10 Warthogs and Apache helicopter attack aircraft armed with surface-to-surface missiles and to ground-based Multi-Launch Rocket System (MLRS) bombardment systems

In order to do this type of work safely and effectively the Special Forces teams need reliable and secure radio communications, sensors and surveillance devices. Modern secure radios can either transmit data or pre-formatted messages in high-speed bursts which are over in seconds using Racal Merod equipment, or they may use frequency-agile or hopping techniques, in which the sending and receiving radios change frequency, simultaneously in a pre-arranged coded pattern.

Aviation and Land Transport

Special Forces may be delivered to their area of operations by foot, lifted by helicopter, dropped by parachute or landed by submarine or small boat.

The US SEALS and British SBS have perfected techniques for exiting from submerged submarines in SCUBA gear, and, after swimming to a target, returning to the submarine. The submarine remains submerged, but deploys a small buoy for the Special Forces team to re-locate its position; the SCUBA swimmer then follows the anchor line of the buoy down to the submarine.

Inflatable assault boats with outboard motors were used during the Falklands War to put Special Forces ashore. The Argentine Special Forces called 'Buso Tactico' had trouble with the thick kelp seaweed when they landed in the initial invasion. On rivers, swamps and inshore waters smaller inflatable boats and canoes allow patrols to make silent approaches to enemy positions.

The Boeing Vertol Chinook can lift vehicles, such as Land Rover 90s and 110s and similar vehicles, as internal loads and insert them deep inside hostile territory. This capability extends the range and duration of operations.

Where hides can be established vehicle patrols can work from a base. The SAS, operating inside Iraq, used tactics similar to those carried out by Second World War SAS teams in North Africa. The SAS teams in World War II, the experienced Long Range Desert Group (LRDG), used specially converted quarter-ton vehicles to ferry them into Axis controlled areas, whereas the men of 22 SAS used Saudi supplied Unimog trucks as 'mother ships'. These bigger vehicles were able to carry greater amounts of stores and ammunition.

During the Gulf War, SAS Land Rovers carried motor cycles which allowed one or two men to extend their range of operations.

Fast Attack Vehicles (FAV) can carry two or three men and owe something of their design to 'beach buggies'. They were used by US Special Forces in the Gulf. These vehicles are low slung, fast and a more stable platform than a motorcycle, being capable of mounting weapons as large as the Browning .50 in HMG. One tactical philosophy has FAVs working with a larger 'mother ship' which carries the food, fuel and ammunition required for each operation.

The size and role of helicopters includes liaison types, deploying a four-man team, which have been extensively used in Northern Ireland. In Vietnam Iroquois (Huey) helicopter crews became adept at inserting small Long Range Patrols (LRPs) close to the Cambodian border or Special Operations Group (SOG) teams across the border. The Black Hawk or Puma have the advantage that their greater range can carry more men and stores. Special Forces may also be backed by the AH-64 Apache attack helicopter. Although helicopters may not carry the same weight, or ordnance, as a fixed-wing attack-aircraft, they are very flexible and, with night vision equipment, can support Special Forces by day or night. During the Gulf War, Apaches were critical in the opening moments of the air war against Iraq by lifting Special Forces to destroy their air defence radars, allowing the Coalition bombers to enter Iraq through a gap in the Iraqi radar cover.

Harley-Davidson MT350 & MT500 Motorcycles USA

Military motorcycles date back to World War I where they were used for liaison and carrying despatches. In World War II the Germans made extensive use of motorcycles fitted with side-cars for reconnaissance.

On increasingly congested roads they have the advantage that military police or despatch riders can weave through the traffic in a way that would be impossible for a HMMWV or Land Rover.

Harley-Davidson, who have made motorcycles since 1903 and military machines since 1917, purchased a British company making an off-road 350 cc machine. They produced an improved version of the 350 cc together with a larger 500 cc off-road bike. Both the American machines looked very similar, with air cooled engines and deep off-road suspension. Though meant to be single-seat machines, a passenger could be carried in an emergency.

Enhancements to these earlier machines include forward pannier boxes, a gun box, convoy lights and blackout switch. The USAF Combat Control Teams use the bigger 500 cc machine which have front and rear panniers, and a handlebar

gun-mount for an M16 and IR night vision headlamp.

The **Harley-Davidson MT500** can be rigged for low velocity airdrops and is fitted with tie-points for securing them to a pallet. The comparatively light weight of the machine means that it can be dropped using a T-10C cargo parachute.

The Special Forces applications for motor cycles include liaison and reconnaissance. The Australian SAS pioneered the technique of carrying a motorcycle on a frame on the back of their 6 x 6 Land Rover 110 Heavy Duty vehicles. In the Gulf War in 1991, 22 SAS used the same technique on their smaller 4 x 4 110 Land Rovers. In some situations the motorcycle was cached to be recovered when the Land Rover patrols had returned from the operation.

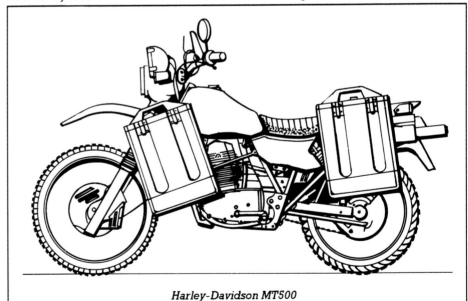

Harley-Davidson MT500

Specification

Harley-Davidson MT350

Engine: Air-cooled, single cylinder four stroke with Electric Start
Length: 2.168 m
Width: 0.790 (across handlebar)
Unladen weight: 152.8 kg
Acceleration: 1 - 106 kph in ten seconds
Water crossing : 0.5 m
Range 320 km with 32 km reserve
Fuel consumption: 93.3 kilometres per 4.54 litres
Manufacturer: Harley-Davidson Inc, Milwaukee, USA

The Harley-Davidson MT500 500cc military motorcycle under camouflage.

Wessex Saker Light Strike Vehicle UK

Following the success of the United States Fast Attack/Light Strike vehicles in the Gulf War, two British companies, Longline and Wessex UK, looked at the concept and produced slightly different designs.

The **Longline Light Strike Vehicle (LSV)** has a VW 1.91 flat-four water-cooled petrol engine, while the **Wessex Saker** has a Perkins Prima 80T 1.993, 4-cylinder, water cooled, turbocharged diesel. Different versions of the **Saker** can carry between two and four crew, whilst the **Longline** is a two seater. In an emergency a Light Strike Vehicle has carried up to 12 soldiers.

Although they are clearly vehicles which are ideal for Special Forces, they can also be used for airfield security and installation defence, where a quick-reaction force may need to reach a remote location at considerable speed, if there has been an incursion.

The maximum load on the **Saker** is 700 kg while the **Longline** can carry 454 kg. The **Longline** has a Universal Mount Interface (UMI) which allows a range of weapons to be installed, such as 7.62 mm and 12 .7 mm machine guns and a 40 mm grenade launcher. The **Saker** being bigger can mount the 30 mm ASP cannon and even the Hellfire anti-tank missile. The **Saker** can tow trailers or the 120 mm mortar. Stowage for the crew's kit is in panniers and racks along the sides of the vehicle.

One of the drawbacks with the LSV concept is that ground clearance can be low: the **Longline** clears 0.3546 m and the **Saker** clears 0.35; however, Wessex point out that a low silhouette is not only protection in the visual range but also against the IR signature of a warm vehicle engine and chassis. The **Longline** and **Saker** present a smaller target and are more agile than a conventional 4 x 4 if they come under fire. They are also light enough to be manhandled if they bog down.

Optional extras for vehicles like the **Longline** and **Saker** include extra fuel tanks, Kevlar armour, GPS, ignition retardant for fuel tanks and run flat tyres.

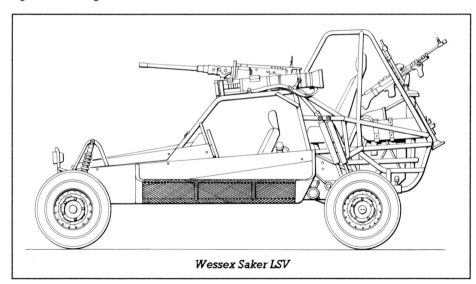

Wessex Saker LSV

Specifications

Wessex Saker

Engine: Perkins Prima 80T water-cooled turbo-charged diesel
Length: 3.9 m
Width: 1.86 m
Height: 1.73 m
Weight: 1100 kg
Side slope: 48 degrees
Turning circle: 12.3 m
Manufacturer: Wessex (UK) plc, Reading, UK

The Wessex Saker (Eagle) 4 x 2 Light Strike Vehicle.

The **Nordac NMC-40 Warrior** is one of a range of low slung 4 x 2 two or three-seater vehicles which were developed in the late 1980s from off-road racing cars.

These vehicles have the advantage of greater stability than a motorcycle, although the crew are as vulnerable to small arms fire. Fast Attack (FAV)/Light Strike/Light Forces vehicles can however mount a range of weapons which can be used in attack or withdrawal.

The big (725 kg) Teledyne Light Forces vehicle has a roll frame strong enough to mount a TOW anti-tank missile. At the other end of the scale the **Chenowth Fast Attack Vehicle** has a payload of only 680 kg but a top speed cross country of 60 to 120 kph.

The **Nordac** vehicle has a maximum speed of up to 161 kph and the Teledyne 113 kph. The combination of speed, low silhouette and cross-country agility are design features which make these vehicles ideal for special forces. The **Nordac** and **Chenowth** vehicles have air-cooled petrol engines, whilst the Teledyne has a turbo-charged diesel. All engines are rear-mounted making them less vulnerable to small-arms fire which also gives the driver and passenger/gunner an unobstructed view to the front. The **Chenowth FAV** has run-flat tyres and a racing-type explosion-proof fuel cell. Many features such as the bucket seats and four point harnesses come from experience in racing-car design.

The **Chenowth FAV** saw action in the Gulf War in 1991 with US Special Forces who led the way into Kuwait. It is in service in two and three seat configuration with the US Navy, Marine Corps and Army.

A three-man vehicle has the advantage that a crew member can stand in the back seat to operate a weapon, a heavy machine gun or grenade launcher; but the penalty is the loss of stowage space for fuel, water, ammunition and rations.

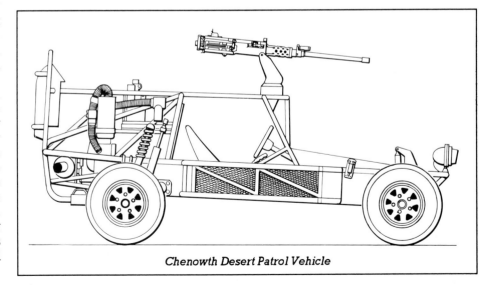

Chenowth Desert Patrol Vehicle

Specification

Chenowth FAV/LSV

Engine: STD 21 air-cooled petrol, 94 HP at 4400 rpm
Unladen weight: 950 kg
Max. speed: 135 kph on road, 60-120 kph off road
Range: 965 km (with auxiliary tank)
Ground clearance: 0.406 m
Manufacturer: Chenowth Racing Products Inc., California, USA

The Nordac Warrior NMC-40 Long-range Fast Attack Vehicle.

Production of the **M151** has ended but it is still in wide use around the world. It was designed to replace the M38, which in turn had replaced the Jeep in US service. The **M151** looks very like the Jeep with its angular mudguards and cut out sides.

The first **M151s** entered service in the US Army in 1960 and were used extensively in Vietnam. As a result of the criticism that the M151 was less stable than the M38, the width was increased from 1.58 m to 1.943 m in the M825, a modified M151A2.

When production finally ceased the AM General Corporation had produced 95,000 vehicles. Besides the utility version there were the M107 and M108 communications vehicles with radios installed in the rear, with a passenger seat facing backwards so that the operator could work the set. The M718 and M181A1 were ambulance versions which had a driver and medical orderly and could accommodate a stretcher and three seated passengers, two stretchers and two seated passengers or three stretchers.

The M825 was fitted with a rear-mounted M40 106 mm recoilless rifle. When the Hughes TOW anti-tank missile replaced the M40, conversion kits were available to bring the vehicle back to M151A2 standard. Ironically, in mid-1987 25 M151A2s were converted to M825 by the US Army in order to meet a requirement from Somalia.

The petrol engine in the **M151** does not now meet emission standards in the USA; but, in the United Kingdom, the firm of AF Budge has developed a re-engining package with a Perkins Prima 80T turbo charged diesel engine. These conversions not only increase range, but give reduced fuel consumption and greater reliability.

Diesel-engined **M151s** may still be in service in the 21st Century since the tough little workhorse is ideal for liaison work and patrolling and is popular with special forces.

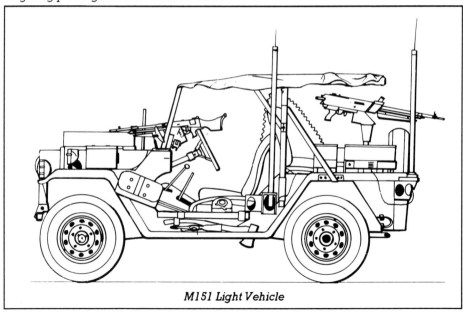

M151 Light Vehicle

Specification

M151

Engine: L-142 4-cylinder liquid-cooled OHV petrol
Length: 3.352 m
Width: 1.58 m
Height: 1.803 m
Weight: 1012 kg
Turning circle: 5.486 m
Manufacturer: AM General Corporation, Michigan, USA

The M151 light vehicle during Exercise Bright Star in Egypt.

Mercedes-Benz 750 kg Light Vehicle   Germany

The **Mercedes Gelaendewagen** known as the **'G Wagen'** has almost become *the* European light vehicle. Manufactured by Peugeot, 15,000 are in service with the French Army as the P4. The French vehicle is powered by either a Peugeot 1971 cc 4-cylinder petrol engine, or a Peugeot 2498 cc 4-cylinder diesel engine. Other European users include Austria, Denmark, Greece (where it is licence-produced by Steyr Hellas SA), Luxembourg, Netherlands, Norway, Switzerland and even in former Yugoslavia where 500 were exported before the country fell apart.

Argentina bought 1200 and when the British liberated the Falklands a number were taken as booty for use by the Royal Engineers mine and explosives clearance teams. British soldiers who were used to the old Series 3 Land Rovers said that they thought that the G Wagen was more like a Range Rover. Like the Range Rover and the Land Rover 90 and 110, the **Mercedes G Wagen** has front and rear coil-springs and telescopic shock absorbers. Both front and rear axles are located by one transverse and two longitudinal control links which produce a very smooth ride over some of the roughest terrain.

The **G Wagen** is available in a standard (2.4 m) or long (2.85 m) wheelbase The layout is conventional with a driver and three passengers and a 1.23 m x 1.52 m cargo area in the rear. The rear seats can be folded forward to give extra space. The floor of the load area is made of sheet steel and is fitted with C-type rails which allow radios to be fitted quickly. The vehicle has a folding-tilt, detachable side-panels and a folding windscreen. A self-recovery front winch may be fitted.

Optional military extras include a radiator and engine guard, brush guards for the headlight, a weapons rack, a hinged spare-wheel carrier, and a frame for a 20 litre fuel container. Weapons include the 106 mm recoiless rifle, Milan ATGW as well as the MG3 and AA52 machine guns.

The **G Wagen/P4** is an ideal vehicle for Special Forces since it is not a signature vehicle and can also be easily serviced and maintained through the existing military logistics chain.

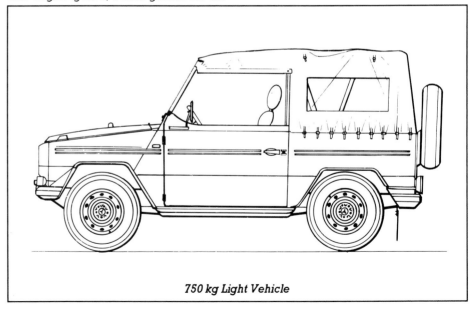

750 kg Light Vehicle

Specification

Standard wheelbase
Mercedes-Benz 750 kg

Engine: OM616 4-cylinder diesel 2404 cc
Length: 4.145 m
Width: 1.7 m
Height: 1.995 m
Weight: 1670 kg
Turning circle: 5.5 m
Manufacturer: Daimler-Benz AG,
Stuttgart, Germany

A Greek built G Wagen produced by Steyr Hellas AG with a 106 mm recoiless rifle.

Land Rover Special Operations Vehicle UK

The Land Rover has long been a vehicle favoured by the SAS. It is a tough and reliable vehicle and carries a good payload. Until recently, existing Land Rover Series 3 Airportable, the 110 or Ninety series vehicles, were modified with extra stowage and weapons-mounts, including smoke-dischargers mounted on the front bumper. After the Gulf War, Land Rover studied these 'in house' modifications and produced their own purpose-built vehicle.

The **Land Rover Defender Special Operations Vehicle (SOV)** is based on the 110, with which it retains a high level of commonality including permanent four-wheel-drive, long-travel coil-spring suspension, transfer box and the latest generation of gearbox, steering and braking systems. It is configured as a long-wheelbase, all-terrain, weapons platform and can carry one or two machine-guns on the central roll bar, the 30 mm ASP cannon or a 40 mm grenade launcher. An extra machine-gun can be mounted in the co-driver's seat. There are extensive racks and stowage bins and these allow the **SOV** to carry a 50 mm MG or 81 mm mortar and ammunition and/or an anti-tank missile. The bins will also

accommodate the crew's kit, ammunition and rations.

The **SOV** can be carried in a C-130 Hercules, or the CH-47 helicopters. It can be carried underslung beneath medium and heavy-lift helicopters and can be para-dropped.

The endorsement for the **SOV** came almost as soon as it had been exhibited: the US Army ordered 60 for their Special

Forces. They had been using the M151 362 kg Light Vehicle which was being withdrawn, to be replaced by the excellent HMMWV, but the Rangers realised that the HMMWV was too wide for some of its uses. The **SOV** proved to be not merely a replacement, but an improvement on the M151, with a bigger payload and a diesel engine, and the right width for narrow passage.

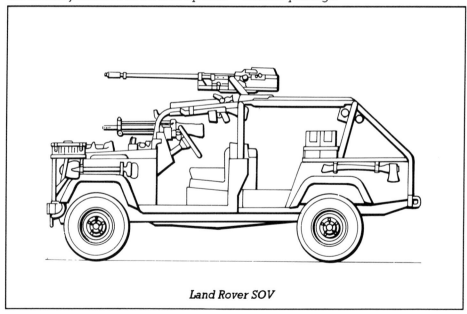

Land Rover SOV

Specification

Engine: 3.528 litre V-8 water-cooled diesel
Length: 4.445 m
Width: 1.89 m
Weight: 3400 kg
Turning circle: 6.4 m
Ground clearance: 0.216 m
Manufacturer: Land Rover, Solihull, UK

The Land Rover SOV in its element on desert patrol.

Land Rover Multi Role Combat Vehicle UK

The **Multi Role Combat Vehicle (MRCV)** uses many of the components in the Land Rover Defender 90 (4 x 4) Light Vehicle and is the company's development of the armed Land Rover as used by the SAS. It is not, however, as specialised as the SOV.

A robust roll-bar cage allows a mounting-ring to be installed which will take weapons such as the 40 mm grenade launcher, 12.7 mm machine gun, Milan anti-tank missile and even the 30 mm ASP cannon. Ammunition is stowed in bins on either side of the rear cargo area. Although the gunner is in a rather exposed position he has a completely unrestricted traverse. In action the **MRCV** crew would operate on the 'shoot and scoot' principle, using terrain and vegetation to camouflage the vehicle as they approach the target, engaging it from cover and escaping before the survivors react.

Personal kit for the three-man crew is secured to the sides of the vehicle and on the front bonnet.

The Defender 90 can be powered by a 2.5 litre petrol engine, a 3.5 litre V-8 petrol, a 2.5 litre naturally-aspirated diesel and a 2.5 litre direct-injection turbo charged intercooled diesel engine. With all military cargo vehicles and armoured vehicles now powered by diesel engines it makes logistic sense for customers to opt for a diesel **MRCV**. Diesel has the important safety feature of a lower flash-point than petrol.

The Defender 90 is part of the family of military vehicles which includes the 110 and 130 all having some common components making maintenance and spares holdings easier. The 90 has the same long travel-coil-suspension and front disc-brakes as the Range Rover and 110. This makes for far more comfortable travel cross-country. The British Army vehicle has a 200 Tdi 2.5 litre direct-injection turbo charged intercooled diesel engine with improvements in power, torque and fuel economy over the engine that was fitted to the first vehicles.

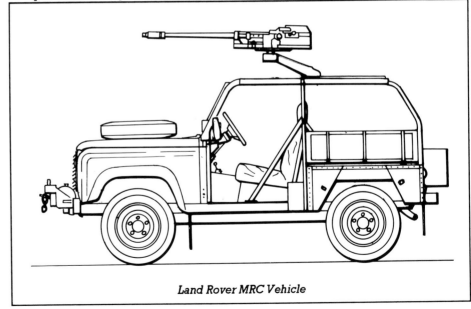

Land Rover MRC Vehicle

Specification

Engine: 2.495 l litre in-line, water cooled turbo-charged diesel
Length: 3.722 m
Width: 1.79 m
Height: 1.993 m
Weight: 2550 kg
Turning circle: 5.75 m
Manufacturer: Land Rover, Solihull, UK

Land Rover Multi-Role Combat Vehicle with 30 mm ASP cannon.

M998 Series HMMWV USA

The **High Mobility Multi-purpose Wheeled Vehicle**, known to many US soldiers as the 'Humvee' was introduced in the late 1980s to replace the M151, and various lighter cargo and utility vehicles. Capable of carrying a maximum load of 1077 kg, the **HMMWV** is more a light truck, rather than a light vehicle. With its wide, low-slung appearance it is an unmistakable vehicle. The width of 2.16 metres and the low centre of gravity make it very hard to roll. In order to ensure a low silhouette, but good ground clearance, (0.41 metres), the transmission runs down the centre of the vehicle, dividing the driver and passenger, but also providing a shelf on which radio equipment or maps can be spread or installed. With power-steering and automatic-gears (three forward and one reverse) the **HMMWV** is easy to drive.

There are a large number of variants, including three TOW carriers, ambulance, cargo, troop-carrier and weapons carrier.

Critics of the **HMMWV** said that it was too heavy and costly. However, during the Gulf War of 1990-91, it proved reliable and tough in the deserts of Saudi Arabia and Iraq. Export orders followed and over 10,000 vehicles have been sold. The biggest order was from Saudi Arabia for 2300 vehicles at the time of the Gulf War; little Abu Dhabi has three!

AM General have a range of modification kits including: up-armouring, spare tyre and jerrican-carriers, driveline skid protection kit, central tyre-inflation system (CTIS) and a special desert operations package which includes secondary oil and fuel filtration, sealed dipsticks, a constant drive fan and enhanced oil filtration. The lightweight weapon station kit is an adaptation of that used on standard **HMMWV** weapons carriers and weighs only 114 kg.

A high mobility trailer (HMT) with a capacity from 680 to 1134 kg has been developed for use with the **HMMWV**. With its on-board capacity and trailer, the **HMMWV** can carry three or four men from a Special Forces patrol with their weapons and equipment in tropical, desert or temperate terrain.

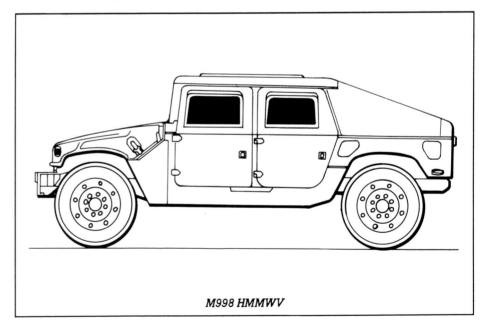

M998 HMMWV

Specification

M1038 Cargo Troop Carrier

Engine: V-8 6.2 litre diesel developing 150 hp at 3600 rpm
Length: 4.72 m
Width: 2.16 m
Height: 1.83 m
Weight, empty: 2295 kg
Range: 482 km
Manufacturer: AM General Corporation, Indiana, USA

The HMMWV is a versatile vehicle which can operate as a cargo, troop and weapons carrier.

Mil Mi-8 'Hip'

The **Mil Mi-8** is a turbine-powered version of the Mi-4 'Hound'. The helicopter was given the NATO reporting name 'Hip'. It has one large passenger door and rear clamshell doors with a hook and winch. It can carry a BRDM wheeled armoured reconnaissance vehicle internally.

The Hip-A first flew in 1961, powered by a 2013 kW (2700 shp) Soloviev turboshaft with a four-bladed main rotor. The type was revised as the Hip-B with five-bladed main rotor and two Isotov TV2-117 turboshafts. The first production model was the Hip-C which introduced Doppler navigation radar and provision for heavy-armament in the defence suppression role.

The **Mi-8** has proved itself an excellent assault and utility helicopter and as a result the type is still built in its upgraded Mi-17 form with an uprated powerplant of two 1454 Kw (950 shp) TV3-117MT turboshafts.

The **Mi-8** has been produced in a number of forms, of which the totals remain unknown. In the early 1980s an estimated figure for both civil and military types was over 7500.

Among the military variants of the **Mi-8** are: the Mi-8 Hip-D, for the airborne communications role; the Mi-8 Hip-E, derivative of the Hip-C, with still heavier air-to-surface armament; the Mi-8 Hip-F, which is the export version of the Hip-E, fitted with AT-3 'Sagger' anti-tank missiles; the Mi-9 Hip-J, airborne communications model; the Mi-17 Hip-H which is the upgraded version of the Hip-C; and the Mi-8 Hip-J and K which are the Electronic Counter Measures (ECM) models.

The **Mi-8** was widely used in Afghanistan to transport Spetznaz special forces. In this theatre it was fitted with IR flare dispensers and extra armament including 7.62 mm and 12.7 mm machine guns. It has also been used in Angola, Nicaragua and South East Asia.

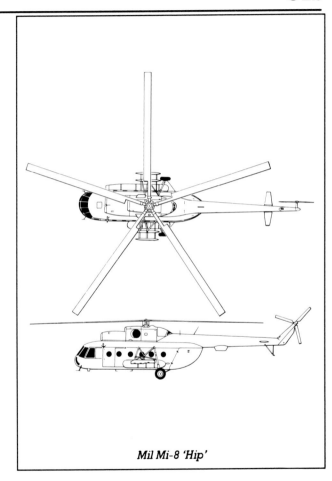

Mil Mi-8 'Hip'

Specifications

(Mi-8 "Hip-C")

Powerplant: two 1270 kW Isotov TV2-117A turboshafts
Length: 25.24 m
Height: 5.56 m
Main rotor diameter: 21.29 m
Weight: take-off clean 11,100 kg
Max. level speed at 1000 m: 260 kph
Service ceiling: 4500 m
Manufacturer: Mil Bureau, State Factories, CIS

Soviet border guards armed with AKS-74 5.45 mm rifles run towards a Mil Mi-8 helicopter.

Eurocopter SA 330 Puma International

Designed in the mid 1960s to meet a French Army requirement for a new medium-lift transport helicopter, the **Aerospatiale Puma** was subsequently produced, in co-operation with Westland in the United Kingdom, to meet also the RAF's need for an all-weather day or night tactical transport helicopter.

The first flight took place on April 15th, 1965 and close to 700 **Pumas** had been built by the time production ended in 1984. Of these the vast majority were unarmed transports. Those built under licence in Romania followed the Soviet/Warsaw Pact practice of mounting anti-tank missiles and machine-gun pods. The Puma gunship, developed in South Africa, which became the basis for the CSH-2 Rooivalk attack helicopter, is fitted with a nose-mounted Helicopter Stabilised Optronic Sight (HSOS) containing Forward Looking Infra Red (FLIR) TV, laser range-finder and autotrack. It is armed with eight ZT3 127 mm anti-tank missiles or up to 72 68 mm HR-68 rockets, plus a 20 mm cannon below the fuselage. The **Puma** was replaced by the Super Puma which first flew on August 13th, 1978; the military variant was given the name Cougar I in 1990.

The French operated **Pumas** in Central Africa, Chad, the Arabian Gulf and Bosnia. RAF **Pumas** have been used extensively in Northern Ireland, Belize, the Gulf and Bosnia. In South Armagh, Northern Ireland, helicopters are used exclusively to transport men and equipment to company bases on the border, since the roads are considered unsafe for troop convoys. South African **Pumas** were used in Namibia and Angola. In a troop-lift role the **Puma** can carry 16 fully-equipped men or 20 men at light scales. In the casualty evacuation (CASEVAC) role it takes six stretchers and six sitting cases. Underslung loads of up to 3200 kg can be carried for short lifts. For Special Forces the **Puma** has the attraction of not being a 'signature' helicopter, so that observers on the ground do not know if it is on ordinary troop or cargo lift operations, or if it is deploying an OP or ambush patrol.

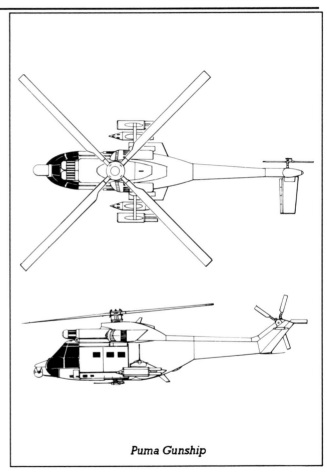

Puma Gunship

Specification

AS 532U2

Powerplant: two 1573 kW Turbomeca
Makila 1A2 turboshafts
Length: 16.79 m
Height: 4.60 m
Main rotor diameter: 16.20 m
Weight, empty: 4760 kg
Max level speed: 327 kph
Service ceiling: 4100 m
Manufacturers: Aerospatiale, France,
Westland, UK

*British soldiers equipped with Milan anti-tank
weapons board an RAF Puma in Saudi
Arabia during the Gulf War.*

McDonnell Douglas AH64D Apache Longbow — USA

Before its combat debut in Desert Storm, the AH64 Apache was criticised for being too complex and maintenance dependent. By the close of the campaign it had been instrumental in the destruction of Iraqi armour, had supported US Special Forces deep inside Iraq and had spearheaded the air-attacks in the Desert Storm phase of operations. Apaches had flown a nap of the earth (NOE) approach into Iraq using Hellfire laser-designated anti-tank missiles and cannon ripping apart the Iraqi radar close to the border with Saudi Arabia.

The Apache first flew on September 30, 1975 and among its numerous features was its ability to stand up to hits from 23 mm cannon. The crew, consisting of pilot and co-pilot/gunner, had a cockpit with armour-proof against 12.7 mm hits. In addition the rugged airframe and landing gear offer a 95.5% chance of impact survival at rates of descent up to 12.8 metres per second. The Black Hole IR suppression system protects the Apache from heat seeking missiles.

The most distinctive feature of the **AH-64D Longbow Apache** is the mast-mounted Westinghouse Longbow radar which, when combined with Hellfire missiles, equipped with radio frequency seeker heads, forms an integrated fire-control radar and missile system making it capable of locating, tracking and despatching targets in the air and on the ground through levels of smoke, rain and fog that would be too much for IR sensors. The Longbow radar scans through 360 degrees for aerial targets or 270 degrees for ground targets, presenting up to 256 targets on the gunner's Tactical Situation Display. Once a target is selected, the Hellfire offers a 'fire-and-forget' capability because it can lock-on to its target before launch and subsequently stay on the target's co-ordinates once in flight.

Deliveries of production standard Longbow Apaches are scheduled to start during 1997 with the current US Army plans calling for some 227 AH-64As. Overseas buyers include the UK and the Netherlands.

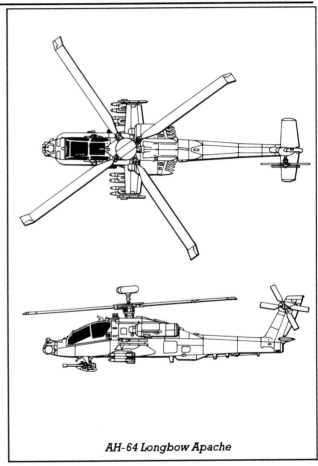

AH-64 Longbow Apache

Specification

AH-64D Longbow Apache

Powerplant: two 1447 kW GE T700 GE-701C turboshafts
Length: 17.76 m
Height: 4.95 m
Main rotor: 14.63 m
Weight: (primary mission) 5552 kg
Max. level speed: 261 kph
Service ceiling: 3800 m
Manufacturer: McDonnell Douglas Helicopter Company, USA

The characteristic Longbow mast-mounted radar is evident on this AH-64D.

Sikorski UH-60 Black Hawk

The **Black Hawk** is the US Army's primary air assault and air movement helicopter. It is a twin-engine, single-rotor, four-bladed helicopter designed to carry 11 to 14 combat-equipped soldiers. The improvement in troop carrying capacity over the UH-1 Huey can be gauged by the fact that 15 UH-60s can do the job of 23 UH-1s.

The first deliveries of 976 UH-60As began in 1978 and continued through to September 1989. In 1989 the introduction of an improved main gearbox and new primary engine produced the UH-60L. The UH-60L has approximately 11% more horsepower. By December 1990, 1071 UH-60s had been fielded by the US Army with plans for a total of 1443 by 1997. New developments for the **Black Hawk** include improved electromagnetic protection, global positioning system (GPS) and secure radio communications (SINCGARS).

The **Black Hawk** has a number of stealth features including low-reflective paint, no visible engine exhaust, crashworthy armoured crew seats, redundant flight-control, hydraulic and electrical systems, de-icing systems, ballistically tolerant main and tail rotor systems, crashworthy self sealing fuel system, and engine and auxiliary power unit (APU) fire detector. Finally it has an infrared suppression system to reduce the IR signature of the engine exhaust.

The **Black Hawk** first saw action in Grenada in 1983 and subsequently in Panama in Operation 'Just Cause', during the Gulf War, in Somalia and in Bosnia as part of Task Force Eagle. In the Gulf in 1991, during Operation Desert Sabre, **Black Hawk**s lifted men of the 101st Airborne (Air Assault) deep into Iraq to seize positions both sides of the Euphrates river valley and block escape or reinforcement routes. It was the largest combat air assault since the Vietnam War.

The Special Operations **Black Hawk** or MH-60K has an upgraded engine, world-wide communications equipment, extended range fuel tanks and equipment for inflight refuelling between helicopters.

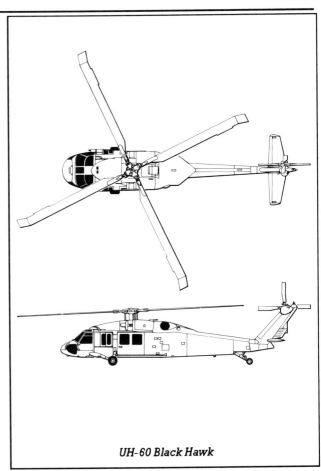

UH-60 Black Hawk

Additional improvements include a totally integrated cockpit which reduces pilot work-load, forward looking IR sensors and improved terrain-following and terrain-avoidance radars.

The MH-60K has a design mission weight of 11,115 kg and a cruising speed of 122 knots. Endurance is 7.6 hours and the maximum unrefuelled self-deployment range with 30 minute reserve is 1215 km. The US Army plans to order 23 MH-60Ks.

Specification

Black Hawk UH-60A

Powerplant: 2 x 1560 hp turboshaft
Length: 15.26 m
Height: 5.13 m
Weight (max): 9185 kg
Max. level speed: 361 kph
Service ceiling: 5790 m
Manufacturer: Sikorski Aircraft Division of United Technologies Corp, USA

A UH-60 Black Hawk dropping Special Forces personnel during a training exercise.

UH-1H Iroquois (Huey)

Universally known as the Huey, the Utility Helicopter 1 or UH-1 is officially called the **Iroquois**. It went through numerous variants before it was replaced in front line service by the UH-60 Black Hawk.

The first **Iroquois** was born as Bell Model 204 out of a US Army requirement in 1955. The prototype first flew in October 1956. In the Vietnam War its strength and flexibility shaped United States Army airmobile operations.

The speed at which men could disembark from the double-doors confirmed the helicopter as a troop-lift machine or 'slick', because its fuselage was smooth or slick. Cross-border operations by the Special Operations Group (SOG) and patrols close to the border by Long Range Reconnaissance Patrols (LRRP) were supported by the tough and versatile **Iroquois**. It was used for 'Dust Offs' - the airborne evacuation of casualties as well as troop -lift and assault.

The Huey Hog was an attack helicopter or gun ship, with machine guns, rockets and grenade launchers. From the Hog grew the Cobra and thence the Apache. From the Huey Slick came the Black Hawk.

The **Iroquois** is still in service with National Guard Special Forces in the United States and is widely used in Europe, South America, Australia and Asia. It is used for inserting police and army anti-narcotics patrols in South America, and for patrolling jungle borders and islands in the Pacific area.

The **Iroquois** has been upgraded with more powerful engines and given 'stealth' features like IR protection for the engine exhaust.

An indication of the vast numbers of **Hueys** still in service can be gained from the total number of 3573 for just one model, the UH-1H, delivered to one customer, the US Army, during the Vietnam War.

Widespread use, as well as the large number of Huey trained pilots around the world, makes it a useful 'sterile' aircraft for some types of covert operations.

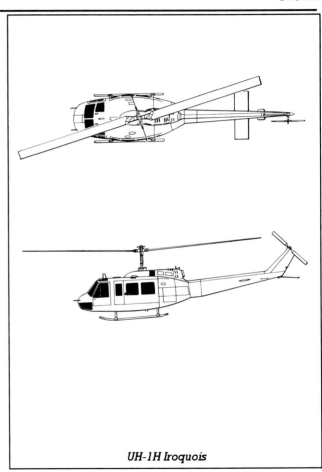

UH-1H Iroquois

Specification

UH-1H

Powerplant: one 1400 hp Lycoming
T53-L-13 turboshaft
Length: 12.77 m
Height: 4.41m
Main rotor: 14.63 m
Weight, empty: 2363 kg
Max. level speed: 204 kph
Service ceiling: 3840 m
Manufacturer: Bell Helicopter Company

A UH-1H helicopter over a US Army training area in Virginia in the summer of 1993.

GKN Westland Sea King

The **Sikoski CH-3 Sea King** first flew on March 11th, 1959. These helicopters set several records for long-distance flights during this period.

During the Vietnam War, CH-3 cargo helicopters were loaned to the Air Rescue Service. Modified for rescue work they were designated HH-3. With extra fuel tanks they could fly from Udom in Thailand or from Da Nang in South Vietnam, reach anywhere in North Vietnam and return home. This endurance and power earned the HH-3C the nickname 'Jolly Green Giant'. Working with Douglas A1 Skyraiders they lifted downed USAF and USN pilots from almost under the noses of the North Vietnamese. CH3Es were used to drop unattended ground sensors (UGS) along the Ho Chi Minh trail as part of the Igloo White operation, monitoring the movement of men and supplies down this axis.

Production ceased in the USA and began, in 1969, at the GKN Westland factory at Yeovil, Somerset, UK. It continues production for both Royal Navy and export customers.

Upgrades to the GKN Westland design include increased payload, reduced fuel consumption and improved reliability. It has a range of over 1400 km. **Sea Kings** are used by the Royal Navy for anti-submarine operations and with airborne radar to provide over-the-horizon cover. In amphibious operations they have been used for troop-lift with 28 fully-equipped soldiers and can carry 3629 kg underslung loads. In an emergency they can carry 42 troops.

Sea Kings were used in the Falkland Islands for troop-lift operations and to bring in 105 mm Light-guns to positions where they could engage Argentinian defences situated around the town of Stanley. Royal Navy **Sea Kings** lifted SAS and SBS patrols into the Falklands. Tragically, it was in a Sea King that the SAS suffered their greatest wartime losses when, on May 19th, 1982, 18 men of D Squadron were killed during a 'cross-decking' operation, between ships of the Task Force, at night; the **Sea King** was hit by a sea bird and crashed into the Atlantic.

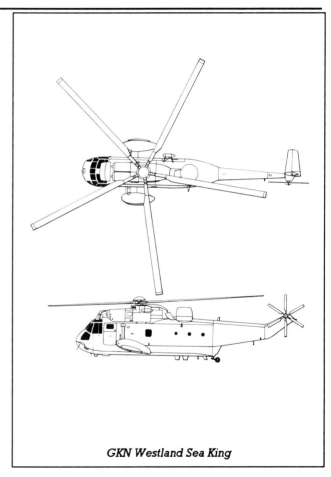

GKN Westland Sea King

Specification

Powerplant: Two Gnome H1400- turbines
Length: 22.15 m (rotors turning)
Height: 5.13 m
Main rotor: 18.9 m
Weight: 5447 kg
Max. level speed: 215 kph
Service ceiling: 3655 m
Manufacturer: GKN Westland, Somerset, UK

Royal Navy Sea King helicopters on ocean-going manoeuvres.

Boeing-Vertol CH-47 Chinook USA

The **Chinook** was delivered to the US Army in 1962 and in 1965 was deployed to Vietnam. It proved an invaluable aircraft for artillery movement and heavy logistics, but was seldom used as an assault troop transport.

Armed **Chinooks**, fitted with two 20 mm Gatling guns, 40 mm grenade launchers and .50 machine guns, were known as 'Go-Go Birds' and were very popular with troops on the ground; however, the experiment proved them to be too vulnerable and was discontinued.

The lift capability of the **Chinook** made it invaluable in the recovery of downed aircraft. By the end of the war Chinooks had recovered 11,500 disabled aircraft worth $3 billion.

Since the Vietnam War, the **Chinook** has become one of the most widely used medium-transport helicopters in the world. A single RAF **Chinook**, the only survivor of helicopters lost on the ship Atlantic Conveyor, during the Falklands War, played a critical part in the British campaign carrying troops and cargo which, at times, were well over its working safe weight.

During the Gulf War, one US Army aviation battalion flew 338 missions, each of 120 nautical miles, into Iraq during the night preceding the main XVIII Airborne Corps attack against the Iraqi positions on the allies' left flank.

A modernisation programme has been running for eleven years which will upgrade 472 early CH-47A, B and C models to 'D' configuration. A special operations version of the **Chinook**, the MH-47E, is entering service with the US Army. It will cruise at 138 knots with a mission weight of 24,494 kg, and have a maximum self-deployment range of 2027 kilometres, with on-board fuel only, including a 30 minute reserve. Endurance is 9.8 hours. The MH-47E can carry up to 44 fully-equipped troops, has a crew of four and is armed with two 12.7 mm machine guns.

The modernisation programme includes new instrumentation which will enable the **Chinook** to fly at night, in bad weather, over extended ranges, using precision navigation techniques.

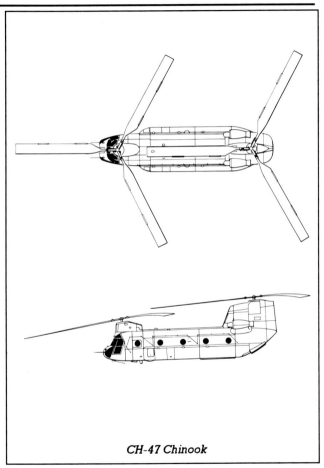

CH-47 Chinook

Specification

CH-47D

Powerplant: 2 x 3750 shp Lycoming turboshafts
Length: 15.54 m
Height: 5.68 m
Main rotor: 18.29 m
Weight: (max): 22,680 kg
Max. level speed: 298 kph
Service ceiling: 4570 m
Manufacturer: Boeing Vertol Company, USA

The lone RAF Chinook, ZA720 which proved invaluable during the campaign in the Falklands in 1982.

Sikorsky CH-53 Sea Stallion

USA

The **CH-53 Sea Stallion** first flew in 1964 and became a major transport aircraft for carrier-borne operations. Capable of carrying 37 troops, it has a range of 869 km. **Sea Stallion** can be fitted with a Flight Refuelling (FR) probe which extends range.

The **Sea Stallion** is operated by the US Marine Corps and US Air Force and was one of the first troop-lift helicopters to have a night flying capability; for this reason it was picked for the dramatic, but unsuccessful, raid into North Vietnam in November 1970, to release American prisoners believed to be held at a camp at Son Tay near Hanoi. Five years later US Marines, flying in **Sea Stallions,** recaptured the US merchantman *Mayaguez* which had been seized by the Khmer Rouge off Cambodia. **Sea Stallions,** towing mine-clearance sleds, were used to clear the mines that had been laid outside Haiphong harbour, as the US government pressured the North Vietnamese to attend peace talks in Paris at the close of American involvement in Vietnam.

In 1980, **Sea Stallions** flown by the US Marine Corps were used by Delta Force in Operation Eagle Claw, in their raid to release the US Embassy staff held hostage by the Iranian Revolutionary Guards. At the air base, Desert One, five helicopters were lost in a refuelling accident and Eagle Claw was aborted. **Sea Stallions** flew troops into Grenada in Operation Urgent Fury in 1983.

Sea Stallions, like the Sea King/Jolly Green Giant, were used for pilot recovery operations in Vietnam. They are currently still used in this role and were deployed by the US Marines and Navy to Liberia to evacuate foreign nationals from the civil war in 1996. Experiments have been conducted to arm them with AIM-9 Sidewinder AAM missiles for self defence.

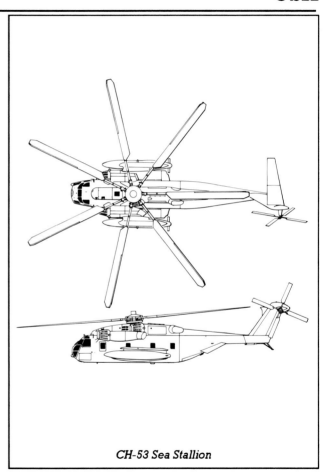

CH-53 Sea Stallion

Specifications:

CH-53 Super Stallion

Powerplant: three GE T64-GE-416
turboshaft engines
Length: 22.35 m
Height: 5.32 m
Rotor diameter: 24.08 m
Weight: 33,340 kg max. (with external
payload)
Max. level speed: 315 kph
Service ceiling: 5640 m
Manufacturer: Sikorski Aircraft Division of
United Technologies, USA

Sea Stallions are readied on deck before Operation Urgent Fury in 1983.

Antonov An-12PB 'Cub-A'

The **Antonov An-12PB** is the Russian equivalent of the C-130 Hercules. As a paratroop transport it can carry 80 paratroops or two BMD tracked armoured infantry combat vehicles. It requires a total of 157 **An-12PB** sorties to lift one, BMD equipped, airborne regiment group. The original concept for the aircraft was the An-10, a four-engined airliner for Aeroflot, which could operate from rough airfields.

The **An-12PB** or 'Cub-A', as it was known by its NATO reporting name, first flew in 1958. Like the Hercules it has an upswept rear fuselage and an integral rear-loading ramp which distinguished it from the Aeroflot civil aircraft. The **An-12PB** has a gun-turret in the tail with two 23 mm NR-23 cannon. During the invasion of Afghanistan Aeroflot aircraft as well as Soviet Air Force transports were pressed into service to move men and material.

A serious drawback of the **AN-12PB** is that its cabin is unpressurised, so that, if it is used for troop lift, its range is seriously reduced because it has to fly at lower altitudes.

The **An-12PB** can carry a maximum of 105 troops or 20,000 kg of payload. It was used to bring Soviet special forces into Prague in the spring of 1968 and into Kabul in December 1979. In soldier's macabre humour, the aircraft that flew the bodies of Soviet servicemen, killed in action in the long Afghan War, were known as 'Zinkies' because the corpses were carried in zinc-lined coffins.

The **An-12PB** has never been used as a gun-ship as has the C-130; but, during the 1965 Indo-Pakistan War, Indian aircraft were used as bombers, operating without loss.

The **An-12PB** has been used in an electronic counter measures (ECM) role and given the reporting name Cub-B. The ECM Cub-C operated out of Egypt, with Egyptian markings, in the 1970s.

The **An-12PB** is still in service in Afghanistan, Algeria, Bangladesh, the Czech Republic, Poland, Russia, Syria and Vietnam.

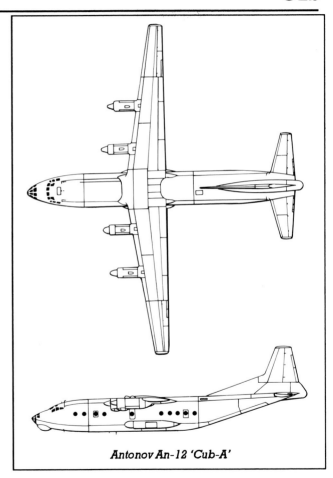

Antonov An-12 'Cub-A'

Specification

Powerplant: four 2984 kW Ivchenko AJ-20K turboprops
Length: 33.1 m
Height: 9.83 m,
Weight, empty: 35,000 kg
Max level speed: 640 kph
Range: (with 10,000 kg payload) 3400 km
Manufacturer: State Industries, CIS

A Czech Air Force An-12PB, during a courtesy visit to the UK, flies along the coast of South Wales

Lockheed C-130 Hercules   USA

The **C-130 Hercules** first flew on August 23rd, 1954 and the first production aircraft was delivered to the US Air Force in December 1956.

Notable design features of the **C-130 Hercules** are: the rear unobstructed cargo compartment; a flat-level floor at truck-bed height above the ground; pressurisation and air-conditioning; full-section rear door and vehicle ramp; turboprop propulsion for high performance; and a modern flight-deck, with all-round vision and retractable landing-gear with 'high flotation' tyres for use from unprepared airstrips.

It has been used as an airborne command and control aircraft, with ground-to-air and air-to-air radio links and as a fuel tanker

In the Falklands War the Argentine Air Force rolled bombs from its rear ramp in an attempt to attack tankers supporting ships of the Royal Navy Task Force. RAF Hercules were equipped with in-flight refuelling probes and carried men and equipment from Ascension down to the South Atlantic.

The **C-130 Hercules** saw extensive service in Vietnam earning it the affectionate nickname 'Herky-bird'.

The gunship variant, designated AC-130, served in Vietnam carrying an awesome armament of one 105 mm howitzer, one 40 mm, two 20 mm and two 7.62 mm guns. Nicknamed 'Spooky' by the US servicemen it was invaluable for long range patrols (LRPS). AC-130s were also in action in the Gulf War attacking Iraqi convoys and positions in Kuwait.

Earlier, Israeli Air Forces **C-130 Hercules** had flown to Entebbe in Uganda to rescue hostages held by German and Palestinian terrorists on July 4th, 1976. The Short-Take-Off and Landing (STOL) capability enabled the IAF to insert the Israeli paratroops and vehicles quickly and at exactly the right locations.

Working with airborne forces the **C-130 Hercules** can drop cargo over the tailgate or paratroops can jump from the side doors.

Though the **C-130 Hercules** can trace its design criteria, as a transport aircraft, back to the Berlin Air Lift and Korean War, the latest version, the C-130J, will be flying well into the 21st Century.

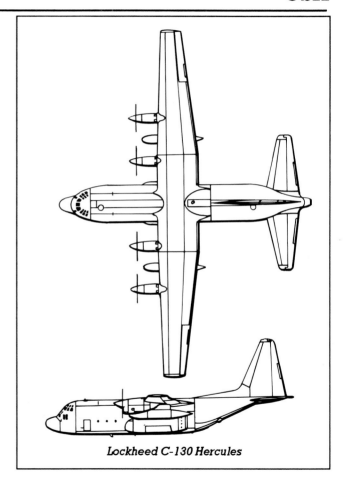

Lockheed C-130 Hercules

Specification

C-130E
Powerplant: Four Allison 4910 hp
T56A-15 turboprops
Length: 29.78 m
Height: 11.7 m
Weight: Empty 33,063 kg
Max level speed: 592 kph
Range: 3895 miles
Manufacturer: Lockheed, Georgia USA

An RAF Hercules takes off from a desert airstrip in Kuwait at the close of the Gulf War.

Irvin Airborne Forces Parachutes   UK

The first experiments with parachutes took place before World War I and by the close of that conflict aircraft, using parachutes, had dropped ammunition to troops in the front line. The inter-war period saw Nazi Germany, Fascist Italy and the Soviet Union develop the first airborne forces. The first operational jumps were undertaken by Soviet forces against 'bandits' in the Caucasus in the 1930s.

The SAS experimented with parachute delivery in North Africa in World War II and have retained their own distinctive parachute wings from that period. Parachutes as a delivery method have been superseded by helicopters in many operations, but they are still useful for inserting forces over long ranges where speed is essential.

The **Irvin** range of parachutes include the Harness Assembly which is compatible with the existing canopy types, the I-32, T-10 and MC1-1B. It has two sets of D-rings for the reserve parachute and weapon/equipment container and a central equipment-suspension-strap with integral jettison device. On the ground the soldier can jettison the canopy and go into action, or clear the Drop Zone (DZ) while still wearing the harness, by using the canopy ground disconnects.

The **Low Level Parachute (LLP) Mk 1** permits fully-equipped soldiers to carry out rapid massed parachute assaults from heights as low as 76 m. The parachute can be deployed at speeds of up to 260 kph from tactical transports.

With an all-up weight of 115 kg the **LLP Mk 1** gives a descent speed of 5.0 metres per second; at 160 kg this increases to 5.9 m/s.

The PR7 Reserve Assembly, which has a contoured base to fit the wearer's chest, can be operated by either hand. It also has a kicker-spring and integral flexible-ring to assist deployment with a net-skirt for increased deployment reliability. In a low-level jump, if there is a malfunction with the main parachute, it is critical that the reserve is deployed almost immediately.

Paratrooper shown in harness with the IRVIN LLP Mk 1 Low Level Parachute Harness Assembly.

Specification

Irvin LLP Mk 1

Weight: 18.5 kg
Length: 560 mm
Width: 430 mm
Depth: 255 mm
Manufacturer: Irvin Aerospace Limited, Bedford, UK.

A stick of paratroops jumping with the Irvin LLP Mk 1 from a C130 Hercules.

SCUBA Equipment

Self Contained Underwater Breathing Apparatus (SCUBA) is used by special forces for infiltration from sea to shore by submarine or small boat.

Using **SCUBA**, shipping, military or industrial targets can be attacked with magnetic charges, 'limpet mines', or conventional plastic-explosive charges. **SCUBA** equipment can also be used by civil and military anti-terrorist forces to search sewers, canals, rivers and etc., prior to visits by VIPs. Should terrorist attacks occur, the special forces will use **SCUBA** to search for evidence, such as discarded weapons or clothing.

Interspiro, a company operating internationally, has produced a self-contained breathing-equipment, in addition to the production of underwater equipment, for use on shore. The equipment, Spiromatic 90 HPBA, is used by soldiers working with unexploded chemical weapons containing lethal agents such as nerve-gas or, for fire-fighting and damage-control teams working on warships or airfields.

For covert diving operations, Interspiro have produced 'Oxydive' - a closed-circuit oxygen system which can be used to a maximum diving-depth of eight metres, with a duration of approximately three hours. Two safety-valves protect both the system and the diver from over-pressure and a lever-operated dosage-valve permits the diver to adjust his buoyancy. Oxydive is silent in operation and releases no gas-bubbles that can be detected on the surface.

The **Divator Mk II** compressed-air breathing apparatus has a new lightweight mask developed in collaboration with the US Navy. This provides much reduced head buoyancy with improved acoustics for line or through-water communications. It includes a valve which flushes the inside of the visor with dry air, keeping it free from condensation.

The **Divator Mk II** has a single-cylinder, or a low-profile twin-cylinder, pack which optimises access to restricted apertures.

The use of composite materials, such as carbon-fibre and Kevlar, has reduced the weight of the new range of cylinders from approximately 45 kg to 17 kg. Interspiro equipment is also in use with Swedish and NATO special forces and anti-terrorist organisations.

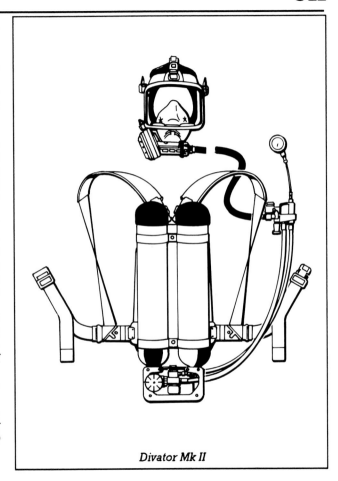

Divator Mk II

Specification

Divator Mk II

Length, single 7 litre cylinder: 590 mm
Diameter: 140 mm
Valve: 60 mm
Consumption rate: 10 to 25 litres air/min.
(slow swimming near surface)
Cylinder pack: 2x4 litre charged at
300 bar contains 2400 litres free air, giving
120 mins. diving
(There are three twin-cylinder packs and
six single-cylinder packs - duration time
varies from 45 mins. to 180 mins. according
to the volume of air)

Manufacturer: Interspiro Limited,
Shropshire, UK

A Special Forces soldier wearing the Divator Mk II diving apparatus.

Rigid Raider   UK

The **Rigid Raider** assault craft entered service with the Raiding Squadron of the Royal Marines in the 1970s, replacing inflatable Gemini craft. It has a cathedral-hull made from glass reinforced plastic (GRP).

The **Rigid Raider's** steeply raked flat bow allows the boat to be driven up shallow beaches and also allows the men on board to disembark very quickly. Brass protective rubbing- strips are fitted to the bottom of the hull and there is built in foam buoyancy. The hull sides have cut-out handgrips, which allow the passengers to hold tight during fast, bouncy, approaches across choppy water. Four lifting-points allow the craft to be transported by helicopter or deployed from larger vessels.

The boat is powered by one or two 140 HP Johnson outboard motors and has a top speed of 37 knots. The **Rigid Raider** is capable of carrying from six to nine fully-equipped men with a coxswain, or a payload of 810 to 1400 kg according to the size of the boat. It can be fitted with inflatable rollerboat seating or preformed aluminium covers fitted over the fuel-bag troughs. The coxswain stands at the stern of the boat to steer, using a wheel

and manual throttle that are mounted on a console.

The **Rigid Raider** is manufactured in two lengths: 5.2 metres and 6.5 metres. For special forces RTK has developed a lightweight craft using Kevlar, which, without the engines, weighs under 500 kg.

In the Falklands Campaign in 1982 the Raiding Squadron inserted reconnaissance patrols and also used **Rigid Raiders** to provide a 'taxi' service between ships in San Carlos Bay. At the close of the campaign they landed men of Boat Troop, D Squadron, 22 SAS and an SBS team on the eastern end of Wireless Ridge in a violent diversionary raid in support of 2 Para's attack on the western end of the feature.

The **Rigid Raider** design is constantly

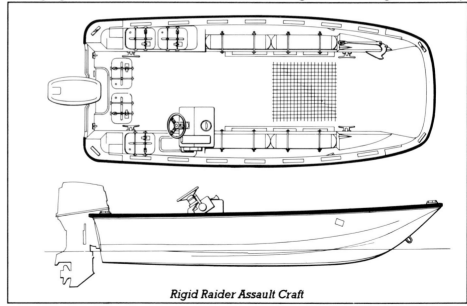

Rigid Raider Assault Craft

being reviewed with new performance and safety features. One new feature is a key and line. The coxswain will have the key attached by the line to his person, the key must be plugged in and switched on to operate the motor. If the coxswain is thrown overboard the motor will automatically cut out.

Specification

Length: 5.82 metres
Beam: 2.2 metres
Height: 1.12 metres
Draught: 0.45 metres
Weight: 800 kg Cox and 6 to 9 troops or 900 kg of cargo
Engine: One or two Johnson 140 HP outboard motors
Top speed: 37 knots
Manufacturer: RTK, Poole, UK

Rigid Raiders operating with special forces in training manoeuvres.

Glossary

ACP:	Automatic Colt Pistol (ammunition)
ATGW:	Anti-Tank Guided Weapon
CIS:	Commonwealth of Independent States (Ex-Soviet Union)
CQB:	Close-Quarter Battle
Delta Force:	US Special Forces modelled on the SAS
Deniable Operations:	Covert operations which, if they are discovered, a government is prepared to deny that it sanctioned
OSS:	Office Strategic Services
ECM:	Electronic Counter Measures
ERA:	Explosive Reactive Armour
GPMG:	General Purpose Machine Gun
GSG9:	German Counter Terrorist Force (literally Border Group 9)
IFF:	Identification Friend or Foe
LMG:	Light Machine Gun
NATO:	North Atlantic Treaty Organisation
NAVSTAR:	US Global Positioning Service Satellite
SAS:	Special Air Service Regiment composed of a reservist element 21 and 23 SAS and the Regular Army Regiment 22 SAS
SBS:	Special Boat Squadron (Royal Marine SF)
SEALS:	Sea Air Land (US Navy Special Forces)
SF:	Sustained Fire
Signature:	The operating sound or appearance which identifies the function or origin of equipment
S & W:	Smith & Wesson
SOCOM:	Special Operations Command (US Forces)
SOE:	Special Operations Executive
SOG:	Special Operations Group
Spoof:	Electronic or pyrotechnic measures to disrupt the guidance of a missile
Spetznaz:	Soviet Special Forces
Sterile:	Equipment which has no makers, names or registered numbers and is in common use, so if captured cannot be traced back to its country of origin
SWAT:	Special Weapons And Tactics
Tandem Shaped Charge:	A shaped charge designed to penetrate explosive reactive armour (ERA)
UNITA:	National Union for the Total Independence of Namibia
UHF:	Ultra High Frequency
VHF:	Very High Frequency
WP:	White Phosphorus (smoke and anti-personnel ammunition)